Bob Eshew — Thanks
for your friendship

Jimmy ____

IT'S TRUE WHAT THEY SAY ABOUT DIXIE

It's True What They Say About Dixie

JIMMY TOWNSEND

Published by
Copple House Books / Caroline House
Road's End, Lakemont, Georgia 30552

Copyright © 1981
by Jimmy Townsend

Standard Book Number: 0-932298-18-4

First Printing May 1981
Second Printing August 1981

Printed for the Publisher by
CHB Printing & Binding
Lakemont, Georgia 30552

To my wife, Geraldine Robinson
My daughters, Kay Maria and Teresa James
And my grandson, Christopher Douglas Vaughn

Contents

Foreword

What words can one use to adequately describe a most unusual author and also a most unusual book? As is so often the case, words are inadequate to properly describe one's feelings about someone else. I find myself in this position with regard not only to Jimmy Townsend the man, but also with regard to the area of our country about which Jimmy writes so vividly.

Mountain people, one of whom I am proud to be, are a different breed. We believe in the worth of other human beings and in paying attention to and giving priority to the truly important things in life. Jimmy does this extremely well in his writings. His background, his experience, his love for the mountains and the people of the mountains all combine to paint a word picture of a most unusual people and regions. Anyone who has ever read anything Jimmy Townsend has written has been filled with an interest in and a knowledge about the mountains. He has a rare talent to be able to describe to other people his feelings and the uniqueness of the people who live in the mountain areas of Georgia.

Anyone who reads this book will have a new appreciation and awareness for the portrayal of places and people in a unique way by a unique personality.

It has been said that "Eagles do not flock, you must find them one at a time." When it comes to writing about the Georgia mountains and its people, Jimmy Townsend is truly one of a kind.

Bert Lance

Way Down South In Dixie

Some Things In Dixie Don't Change

"Is It True What They Say About Dixie?" was a very popular song in the thirties. I suppose for the most part, the song was fairly accurate back then, and it could be said that the same holds true today for a good many things.

A great many people from Scotland settled these mountains of north Georgia between 1700-1800. Old tombstones and land deeds bear such names as McClure, McHan and other "Mc" names. There are also many blacks with these names today that their ancestors probably got from the Scots.

The Scottish people who got here first started Presbyterian churches, which was their religion back in the old country. Churches were built, but as the years rolled onward, settlers merged with other churches which were mostly "foot-washing Baptists" at the time.

J.T. McTavish is a descendant of an early settler, and he still lives on a one-horse farm in the wilderness. He keeps to himself as much as these modern times will let him. J.T. (initials only) still talks a lot like the inhabitants of Scotland today.

When he refers to himself, it is always, "a body can't do this" and "a body can do that," just like the Scottish song "When A Body Meets A Body Coming Through The Rye."

McTavish got on the subject the other day about preachers politicking in the pulpit. "They can't see the hump on their own back," he said matter-of-factly. He told of his favorite grandson and his wife moving to the city a few years back.

The couple never "took any stock" in church until a child was born. The couple started going regularly to a Baptist church that was about as close a thing to the mountain churches that they could find.

His grandson became a deacon, and the church doors couldn't open without him and his family being there. This was true for any in-between functions as well as the Sunday service.

"They enjoyed their religion," J.T. said rather sadly, "until the devil got ahold of the preacher and he began politicking for a certain candidate for President right from the pulpit."

It so happened that McTavish and his clan were supporters of the other man running for President. "An umpire," said J.T., "will have half the crowd against him, no matter how he calls the play."

You could see the Scottish blood boil as the veins popped out on J.T.'s neck. He went on to tell how the preacher got so sickening that he suggested to his congregation that they contribute to the campaign of his choice for President.

The kids didn't try to stir up anything with the other members, but they did quietly leave the church. Much to McTavish's disappointment, his grandchildren have never started back to church anywhere. "They loved their church," he said, "but there was this little matter of principle."

J.T. McTavish was all strung out now. He told how preachers had been immune from criticism, no matter how they call the play. He was saddened that the preachers had left themselves open to be examined on what they say in the pulpit among other things.

He went on to tell of many crooked things that he knew that some preachers had done, and people turned their backs because the preacher was doing the Lord's work, one way or another.

"They," he said, "are not any longer for separation of church and government, so they and their churches will probably be paying taxes in the future. The churches are big business—apartment houses for rent, even loan sharking, yet they escape the tax burden that the rest of us have to face. Most of them nowadays are more for themselves than they are for saving souls."

Maybe old J.T. is right, only time will tell, but it is my opinion that preachers, like politicians, entered their profession with the best of intent. Somewhere after that, some of them become greedy and corrupt. "They will fix it," Mc said, "with some folks, but the devil can quote scripture to suit his own purpose."

Quarreling still goes on in the churches as it did in the thirties. Turnip greens, okra and cornbread are still a favorite for weekday meals with a lot of folks. Sunday dinner is fried chicken and banana pudding.

The biggest change in the South is industry replacing "King Cotton." But if you start adding things up, "It's true what they say about Dixie."

Try To Keep Up With Silas McDougell

Silas McDougell lives up in the mountains as far as you can go by automobile. The road stops at his house just short of a steep mountain bluff. A beautiful clear creek which Silas built a bridge over many years ago flows almost down through his yard. It's a typical mountain home—never been painted—that has a barn and a crib out back. A well traveled path goes down to a little outhouse at the edge of the back yard.

A water moccasin slithered off the bridge and into the water as I drove across the bridge. The loose boards sounded like distant thunder as the wheels touched them. Four dogs came charging around the house as I pulled up in front of the house. The barking and growling of the dogs sounded about as savage as anything you can hear in the mountains.

Silas came out on the porch and yelled to the dogs, "Shet up! —hush, I said." They quietened down a little but whined nervously at my intrusion there in Peaceful Valley. "Light," he said, "light and come in." As I walked up the steps to the porch he said, "Pull you up a cheer and rest a spell." I sat down in the old rocker which looked like it had seen several bottoms, the last one made out of an old inner tube.

Clementine, his wife, came out on the porch. "Hide do" she said politely. I offered my hand but she quickly put it behind her. I remembered that men and women didn't touch flesh in these parts unless they had a right. She was dressed in the old mountain style with a bonnet on her head, long dress with an apron tied around her waist. The apron seemed unnecessary since her dress and apron were already filthy. She went back into the house and soon the up and down thudding of a churn dasher came floating out in the mountain air.

Silas is a big man, about six feet, five inches, weighing in at about two hundred and ninety. He stood as erect as a general and sat down on the porch steps. "Your bottom corn is pretty," I said, looking at the stalks now about knee high. We talked about a good many things, important and unimportant, and the talk turned to

religion. Talk always turns to religion with Silas. His dogs' names
are Matthew, Mark, Peter and Paul. Their cow is Jezibel, and he
calls one of his mules Judas, and the other Moses. Their names
suited. Judas would switch around and kick anything near him,
and Moses looked gentle enough, probably because he was so old.
Three sons by the first wife were Jeremiah, Luke and Daniel. Two
girls by the second marriage were Georgia and Virginia. Their brothers were Nebraska, Kansas, Montana and Nevada.

Silas started talking; he claims to be a Bible Christian. He
doesn't believe in denominations and church organizations and
church literature. He says preachers should not take money for
preaching, that it's a grace from the Lord, and they ought to make
their living in a common way like the Apostle Paul did. He says
that denominations go against the Bible, and organized churches
are just "adding to the Bible."

I was glad when the dogs dragged a rabbit into the yard. This
changed Silas' talk to hunting. One of the dogs came up on the
porch and shook creek water on me. I tasted dog, but at least Silas
was through talking about high paid preachers.

"The panthers are back," he stated flatly. He heard something
like a woman scream the night before. The dogs whined and ran
under the house and hid. Later in the night he heard the sound of
a baby crying. "It's panthers," he said matter-of-factly.

It was almost dark when I left Peaceful Valley. "It's more like
'Lonesome Valley'," I said to myself. I thought about the panther
and locked the doors to the car. I passed the family cemetery
shaded by two big cedars. I looked at the beautiful corn in the
bottom and wondered how Silas could keep farming at his age. All
of his children are long dead. He has outlived three wives. The
current one is the fourth.

The twenty acres of little pine seedlings that Silas set out last
March were shining on the hill. Silas was born in 1878, and in
August he will be one hundred and two years old.

A Legend From Detroit To The Grave

Avery was a little older than me so he must have been about eighteen when he went north via a freight train during the summer of 1938. He was gone about four months before returning home by the same method of transportation. He told some interesting stories about working in an automobile factory and how he had been promoted to a foreman's job in one month's time. He was in the big money, he told us, but got homesick and decided to return to the mountains of north Georgia. He had plenty of money in a bank in Detroit but he just happened to like to ride freights.

What we noticed most about ol' Avery was the change in the way he talked. No Yankee could do it better, and his father was mighty proud of him. They would come down to the drugstore together where about everybody in town hung out. Avery's daddy would grin proudly as he told his son to talk a little for us. He did a fine job of it and he started every sentence with our Savior's name. "Christ," he would say, "don't yez guys get tired of this little hick place?" And then he would spout his foreign Yankee language out a mile a minute. It was amazing how much ol' Avery learned in four months' time.

This was only the beginning for the great adventurer because Avery's daddy told us one day that he had gone down to Florida to manage a big hotel for a millionaire friend at Miami Beach. We wondered about that, too, for Avery never would waste his time over at the schoolhouse like the rest of us boys did.

Along in December and shortly before Christmas we heard the train blow and some of us walked on down toward the depot which had become a habit during the Big Depression. The snow was about five inches deep and we hurried on inside the depot to gather around the pot-bellied stove to keep warm. Looking out the window we saw the freight with a man wearing a hard-brimmed straw hat riding on top of one of the cars. When Avery got down off the train he was sporting white shoes and had a walking cane in his hand. He spoke and went strutting off through the snow towards his father's home about a mile back down the tracks.

He hung around the drug store for the next few days wearing his straw hat and white shoes and the snow hadn't even begun to melt. He could twirl that cane around his finger and toss it up into the air, catching it behind his back as it came down like nobody's business.

Avery wore those same clothes until spring until the medicine show came through. The doctor in the medicine show called for volunteers to come up on stage and assist him in his act. Avery hopped up on that stage like he owned the show. Later while the doctor, who said that he graduated from Harvard University, began playing the banjo, ol' Avery delighted us with a buck and wing dance. The doctor, who said that he came South for his health, must have liked him because when the show left town, Avery went with it.

We had one of those "Wild Man From Borneo" shows to come to town one day. Some horses pulled the cage with the wild man in it. As the wagon went down the main street the wild man would hammer on the bars and growl the fiercest growl you ever heard. It would make chills run up and down your back. Long black hair from the wild man's head dragged the floor.

Bud Pickett and I followed the show on down to the fair-grounds where they were going to set up. As we neared the cage of the "Wild Man From Borneo," a loud roar came from the cage and we ran out to the street, all out of breath before we stopped and looked back.

I heard a voice say "Hi Jimmy. Hi Bud," and then as the hair came off in the wild man's hands he said, "for Christ's sake, don't you know me?" It was Ol' Avery.

I went to Avery's funeral recently. He died in the Veterans' Hospital in Atlanta. All of his folks had long passed on, so no one was there but five of us. There wasn't but one wreath of flowers, which the undertaker had supplied. We talked about it as the preacher left and decided that was the way Avery would want it.

Somehow I didn't sleep much that night, and when the florist opened next morning I went over and bought a small wreath thinking it was the least that I could do for a legend like Avery. When I got to his grave there were four more wreaths placed neatly on the red clay.

A Grandson And Country Memories

When our grandson, Chris Vaughn, age six, visits us, we try to entertain and please him as if he were the president of the United States. Chris watches *The Dukes of Hazzard* on television, and he likes to ride dirt country roads. This kind of road is hard to find in our mountain country this day and time, but there is one above the farm where I was raised which runs for several miles into the next county.

We ride a while before stopping the car to get out to walk a while. I like to watch him run up the banks and back down again into the road. Sometimes he will get away ahead of me before turning around and waving. I suppose I get back in my childhood just watching him.

We moved to the farm in January, 1931, when I was about twelve. The mining town of Ducktown, Tennessee, where we moved from was made up of all kinds of folks, both educated and uneducated. The schools in Ducktown were good, and we may have been somewhat more advanced in worldly things than our new peers who were used to a one-room school, and a teacher for seven grades. We had a radio back in the mining town, too, something that people didn't have in the country where we moved.

Dad bought us a battery radio and a kerosene-burning refrigerator. We had aladdin lamps, and if a fly touched the mantle (burner) it was so fragile that it came to pieces. These lamps put out better light than the wick lamps. Folks would fill up our parlor on Saturday nights to listen to the Grand Ole Opry. It was the tobacco chewing that I couldn't get used to, because a lot of spit was directed toward our whitewashed fireplace. I remember one man who could spit a curve.

Ask somebody how he was and he usually replied, "jest tolerable," and if they spoke first it was usually a big "hide do." An alcoholic was unheard of; if there was someone in a family who got drunk he was referred to as the one "bad to drink." Some would refer to a baby as "hit's purty." "Hit" was always the word for it with most country folks.

We hadn't lived in the country long before we found out that everybody was kin somehow or another, so this eliminated a lot of gossip. Kin were claimed up through the fourth cousins.

It didn't matter what kind of misfortune fell on someone, it was turned off "as the Lord's will," and if someone made a promise he always hedged it with "if nothin' happens." Women with babies were referred to as carrying the "infants on their hip," and families visited often, "taking the day" with one another.

When voting time came, the man with a large family got a lot of attention from the politicians, sometimes getting a sack of flour for free. Occasionally there would be a man who could deliver a whole clan of votes, and he would live "high on the hog" for a few days after an election. This is still true to some extent.

If someone were sick he was "puny" or just felt "porely." If he felt good he was in his "high oats." If he was sick enough to stay in bed he was "bad off." "By rights" was an expression that was used then and still is. "By rights" it ought to be this way, or "by rights" it ought to be plowed again.

We also had the only car in the settlement, and it was on the road most of the time taking someone to the doctor or even to see some sick kin, sometimes miles away. My brother did the driving, and nobody ever had any money for gas, so this just naturally came out of dad's pockets. I never heard him complain though.

We had a mule and sometimes two. One of the mules would head for the barn at twelve o'clock, taking rows of corn with him. We learned to take out a half hour earlier. One mule would go into fits if he saw a whiskey bottle. His former owner was "bad to drink" and would beat the mule when he was drinking. Every stick one mule saw would make him rare up and snort. He took the sticks to be a snake. He was bitten once and nearly died.

"Wake up! Granddaddy, let's go!" Chris was pulling at my sleeve. I took one last look as we got in the car. All these changes in people and even places have been brought about by a little box called television. Everybody now is in contact with all parts of the world by this invention and I'm glad. "Make some dust, Granddaddy!" I put on my brakes and the dust covered the sight of the road. He laughed as we headed home.

Don't Step In The Hoya

We had visitors out on our patio the other day and if someone had come up while we sat there he might have thought he was on an Indian Reservation. They were cousins of mine, Big Jim Reece and his sisters from Rome, Georgia.

All of my mother's people look like Indians, more so than some who live on reservations. There is a reason for this according to Big Jim: our great-great-grandmother was Chief Bird's daughter. The chief headed a tribe of Cherokee not far from where I live now, but he was so particular that he disowned his daughter for marrying a paleface.

An uncle of mine and I were up at the reservation at Cherokee, North Carolina one day messing around and saw this chief in full headdress having his picture made with the tourists for a five dollar fee. I borrowed the chief's headdress and put it on my uncle and he looked more like the real thing than the guy in the business. So much, in fact, that the tourists wanted their picture made with my uncle. This displeased the chief so much that he told us to get lost. I wanted to go down to the end of the street and go in business for ourselves, but my uncle wouldn't go along with it.

There is always someone coming by tracing down the Townsends. Dad knew that his folks came from Manchester, England. Mama always had an answer for anyone who bad-mouthed the Indians. "The Whites settling America were running away from their debts."

Jim Reece is six feet five with high cheek bones and copper colored skin. He is now eighty-three years old, but handles himself mentally and physically like a young man. His favorite story is about the young congressman paying a visit to an Indian Reservation in Arizona. He made a fine speech full of promises of better things. "We shall see," he said, "a new era for Indian opportunities." To this the Indians gave a ringing cry, "HOYA, Hoya!"

Encouraged, the young congressman continued, "We promise better things like schools and technical training.". . ."HOYA, Hoya!" exclaimed the audience with much enthusiasm. "We pledge better hospitals and medical assistance," said the congressman. . . . "HOYA, Hoya!" cried the Indians.

With a tear running down his cheek the congressman ended, "We come to you as equals, as brothers, so trust us.". . .The air shook with a long mighty, "HOYA, Hoya!"

Greatly pleased by his reception, the congressman began a tour of the reservation. "I see you have fine breeds of stallions and bulls," he said. "May I get out of the jeep for a closer look?"

"Certainly, come this way," said the chief, "but be careful not to step in the hoya."

The Good Ole Days Of Flies

We like to think of the good old days, without being reminded of the bad ones. Ted Hobble says people have rocks in their heads when they long for by-gone days. In his youth, milk sold for a nickel a quart, delivered. You couldn't buy it at the stores. Some of the milk tasted like the weeds that the cow ate. Most folks, according to Ted, had a cow. They had a barn on the back of their lot where the cow lived. Right next to the barn was a manure pile. There were also several million flies that lived in the barn and divided their time between the manure pile and the house. They came to the house for a visit and then returned to the manure piles.

Now Ted's folks had screen doors, a luxury that some folks did not. But he went to on say that there was always some accommodating person who would open the doors to let the flies in.

Three or four children who had to go out and in two or three times a minute, and the neighbor who came in to borrow something. Her gossip started about the time she was leaving. She would talk and hold the screen door open for twenty or thirty minutes. I know some folks today who don't know how to talk through a screen door.

Hobble said, "You might get the idea that the people did not mind the flies. You couldn't be more wrong. We hated them. We did everything we could to discourage them, except get rid of the barns and the manure piles. Some homes had a long stick suspended from the ceiling over the table. From this stick hung long streamers of newspaper. This contraption was waved back and forth at mealtime to keep the flies on the wing. This kept them from being drowned in the gravy or getting their feet all greasy in the butter, but it didn't make for fewer flies."

But most of us here in the mountains can remember the tanglefoot, a sticky paper. You laid it around in strategic positions and hoped the flies would get caught in it. When a fly landed on it, that was the end of the fly.

A toddler would reach up on the table to see what he could reach, and sometimes he reached the tanglefoot. Of course, it stuck. Then he would try to pull it loose with the other hand, and that would get stuck, too. Then he usually tried to wipe the stuff off on himself or some furniture, but was never completely successful. Heck, he never did get rid of it until some adult came to his assistance; and by then, he and the house were in a mess.

Then there were the long rolls of this sticky stuff hung from the ceiling, in the hopes a fly might have an accident in flight. It smelled worse than the manure pile and sometimes, when some tall person walked through the room in the dark, you could hear some mighty loud curse words.

On the back porch, there was a fly trap made of screen, about a foot high, and three feet in diameter. The flies were coaxed under the thing with a pan of sugar water. When they flew up, they were caught in the trap. Millions of their friends came to see them and sat and flew around the outside of this cage until someone opened the kitchen door and let them in the house. There were always more flies outside than there were in the trap.

On days when there was company, after dinner (the noon meal), all the women in the house would cover the food and darken the dining room and kitchen. Then they would start at the back of the room and wave dish cloths frantically in the air and scare the flies out through the back door. Whatever a person did to eliminate flies, there were always plenty left in the house. It was impossible to sleep in the daytime. This, I think, is why people got up early and went to work early.

There was an advantage to all this. The flies always knew when it was going to rain. They covered the screens and porches, and would bite as hard as a mosquito, raising welts as big as a walnut.

Mr. Poole And His Country Store

Far out beyond Atlanta's lights, away from the hustle and the roar, the crickets chirped on summer nights beneath the country store. The dry-goods boxes scattered about were welcome seats for the weary farmers of the soil who would gather there on evenings. A swinging sign of Coca-Cola was right above the door. It was said that Will Poole was the owner of this store.

This was the way it was when Will Poole opened his store in a two-story brick building in Jasper in 1932. It was one of the older buildings in town, having been built shortly before the turn of the century. This building and Mr. Poole would become a legend for what happened there during the next forty years.

The time of the beginning of the country store was during the Great Depression. Poole sold the farmers fertilizer, seed, clothing and food on time, to be paid when the crops were gathered in the fall. It was a rare case indeed if anyone was turned down for credit. Poole was described as a godsend to the mountain people of that time, where there were very few jobs and not much money.

He had anything in the store that anyone might need, everything from brogans to tweed. Silks, dresses and gingham bright were spread before customers from morning until night. Tea, sugar, coffee, molasses, grindstones and coal tars. Suspenders, soup beans and fruit jars . . . .

Amazing as it may sound, the store prospered, even during the depression, and a funeral home was added upstairs in the building. Many a person whose family couldn't pay for it was buried by the Poole Funeral Home; a poor person's funeral was carried out the same way that the funeral was of someone who could pay. Then furniture was added in the store. People will say today that Will Poole put them in housekeeping when they didn't have a dime.

Time moved right along as the store carried fine combs, rakes, hoop cheese, paints, rice and looking glasses. Saddles, horse collars, dishes and seed for grasses. The forties rolled around, and Will Poole would sell appliances to a couple and charge it to them just like he would a sack of flour. Then he watched kids who grew up around his store go off to do battle. "No one is to be sent a statement for the duration" was his order.

Come November 1960, he was elected to represent Pickens County in the state legislature. Back roads were paved. Young folks from Pickens were given state jobs, something that seemed impossible. He carried hundreds of folks to the state Capitol, even bought their dinner. Everyone knew that it cost Will Poole money to be a state representative. "Old Marv," Jim Gillis and Jim Peters knew that we were up here. Representative Poole saw to it. He served for ten years.

He died a couple of months ago. I meet people on the street, and they tell me that they wish they had given Mr. Poole "flowers while he was living." Some remarked that their families would have starved to death if it hadn't been for Will Poole.

The old store has now been renovated, and there is a modern variety store in the building. But every time I pass there I recall the early days when I hung around there as a boy. Umbrellas, lamps and lamp globes, Octagon soap, scythes, hats, overalls, boots, balogna and bacon. Thread, nutmeg, pins and Rough on Rats for cash—but produce and eggs were taken. Underwear, face powder, matches, trace chains and a lot more were found in heaps, stacks and piles in my Uncle Will's country store. He was my mother's brother, and I, too, wish that I had given him flowers while he was living.

Of Trains, Children And Leo

The mountains are approaching their annual coming-to-a-head time. The feeling is transmitted to both animals and people as a nagging impatience to get things brought in for the winter. No one in the mountains escapes it. Not even people who are retired and maybe too old to work. The feeling for this time of year remains until the end.

I walked down to the garden to pick over the few remaining vegetables when the whistle of the freight over in town came floating through the near-autumn atmosphere. I stopped and listened, to see if the train was going to stop over in town. There are only two freights a day through Jasper now, but it's easy to recall when three passenger trains went up and three went down. There were about four or five freights a day back then. People set their clocks by them.

I heard the clickety-clack of the wheels pass under the overhead bridge that hobos used for a shelter years ago. The sound of the empty boxcars are fading in the distance. Empty boxcars are noisier than flat cars that are loaded. "It's not going to stop," I said aloud as I heard the sound of the caboose wheels go through town and on toward Tate. The engineer was "setting" down on his old-fashioned whistle down at the crossing, a sound that can make you feel mighty lonely this time of year.

My grandson, Chris Vaughn, started his first year of public school down at Murdock in East Cobb County the other day, and as I watched him get on the bus it brought back the memory of a friend, a newspaper columnist who passed on some time back.

Leo Aikman always wrote a column about children beginning school this time of year. It was usually a humorous piece about the little children he loved so much. The teacher in Brooklyn said, "Johnny, give me a sentence using the word "bewitches." After deep thought Johnny said, "Youse go ahead, I'll bewitches in a minute."

29

Leo knew what it was to go to school in a two-room school-house. He knew what it was to walk three miles to school in two or three feet of snow. He knew the tingling of the toes as he took off his shoes around the wood heater to get the feeling back in his feet. Leo knew what it was to teach school, as this is what he was doing when he left his home state of Indiana to come to Marietta and oversee Kennesaw Park for the government.

We talked about this a lot, about a Yankee coming South for such a job during the times when some Georgians wouldn't wear "blue" overalls, much less be courteous to a Yankee. I asked him one day how he got by, and he told me due to his talking so much like a Southerner he was never asked where he was from. "They just took it for granted," he said, "that I was just another Georgian."

Leo would later join *The Marietta Journal* and then *The Atlanta Constitution* and became a most beloved columnist.

There was the six-year-old boy in school for his first day when the teacher asked him if he knew his ABCs. "Hang no!" replied the lad. "I've just been here one day," was another of Leo's favorite school children jokes. And then the sign near a school-house: "DON'T KILL OUR CHILDREN" . . . underneath scrawled in a child's handwriting, "Wait for a teacher."

Iris, Leo's wife, still lives in Marietta. Susan Hughes, his only child, is news editor with *The Marietta Journal*, and today's column is dedicated to them as Leo's favorite time of year approaches.

Will The Passenger Trains Come Back?

Several times a day now someone will ask with hope and wishfully, "Are the passenger trains coming back?" The people my age and some even younger are hungry to hear the cindery screech as a locomotive slid into the depot, the whistle and the door sounds, the ceremony of boarding — few children today can imagine what complex excitements these events once aroused.

There was a time in these mountains when the trains provided all the excitement that was needed. Folks in small towns met trains, sometimes crying with gladness as their relatives got off the train. You would often see a merchant take his watch out of his vest pocket, look at it, and with the chain dangling put the watch back. Then he would close his doors, put up a "back in 30 minutes" sign before hurrying down toward the depot as we heard the train whistle "coming up the grade."

Gerald Owens was about my age, and we knew that his daddy was killed by a train when Gerald was a baby in 1919. There was talk. There always is. Some said that "Deadhead Owens," who was bad to drink, was killed and put on the tracks. The night passenger rounded the curve before the light of the train picked up Deadhead, they said. The engineer said that he was lying in the middle of the tracks and looked like he was asleep. Some said that Owens was drunk and went to sleep on the railroad. Others said different.

Gerald, too, went to work on the railroad. He got a job as a fireman in 1939, and during the war years was promoted to engineer. We heard how Jerry would blow the train whistle long and lonely as he passed the place where his daddy died. Nobody was going to forget his daddy, and nobody has until this day. There is still some talk.

Gerald didn't go in the army. The government needed him to drive trains. We heard about him coming out of Corbin one night blowing that whistle. People playing cards stopped to listen, they said. Folks on the streets stopped and listened to the long wailing of that train whistle. They still heard it on down the mountain, but the fast running freight didn't make the curve. Later it was in

31

the papers how Gerald told his fireman to jump. Gerald rode the train to his death.

I was in Missouri last summer and stopped in a "jerkwater town" for gas. I noticed the old train over at the depot across the street, and as I always do when I see a train, moved closer. There was this man dressed in overhauls, a bandana around his neck and wearing an engineer's cap that looked like my grandson's.

He was giving the history of trains and was doing a good job of it. I listened as he told how "jerkwater" towns came to be called that. Locomotives often pulled into a town that had a water tank and little else. A crewman would jerk a cable to lower the nozzle to the boiler of the steam engine. The little places came to be called "tank towns" and of course "jerkwater towns."

A lot of our language was handed down to us by railroad men according to the guide. When a train "made the grade," or a steep hill, all of the train breathed a sigh of relief. When a person achieves something today we speak of his "making the grade."

Some of the train language came from sailors. "All aboard!" is nautical talk as are "berth" and "crew." "Coach" and "station" came from the stagecoach language and went into the railroad talk. Sports fans who attend "doubleheaders" may not know that to railroad men the term denoted a heavy train pulled by a pair of locomotives. A "deadhead" was not an ignorant person, but a passenger who, by special privilege, rode for free. Later on, the term was applied to a freight car returning empty. He went to on explain that "sidetracked" used today means a delay, but then it meant parking your train on a sidetrack so another train could pass. This took up time and some engineers complained of this, but there was no choice.

It was the way the man went to all kinds of trouble to explain about "deadhead" that caught my attention. He emphasized the explanation of the term so much that I moved up closer to him for a better look. It was when he told the few people there that his grandfather, and later father, were called "Deadhead" that I knew who he was.

Melvin Owens' father was killed in that freight in Kentucky when Mel was a baby. "I never knew him," he told me, "but I've heard that he was great."

"He was great," I replied.

We walked together over to the restaurant for a cup of coffee. A cafe with walls reeking with stories from railroad men. I asked Melvin, "Will the passenger trains be back?"

"Of course they will," he replied. "We can't do without them much longer." He went on farther and said, "I'm going to be on the track for as long as I can," and then his voice trailed off. "I'll die on the railroad," he said.

I've thought about it ever since that hot day last summer in a "jerkwater town" in Missouri. I'll think of "Little Deadhead" until I hear from him again, but I can't help but wonder if I ever will. Anyway, I'll always remember the song that he was singing as he walked slowly back to the old train. "All Around the Water Tank, Sleeping In The Rain. A Thousand Miles Away From Home. Just Waiting On A Train."

Just A Little Bit South Of North Carolina

A Checkered Apron

A while back, we mentioned the apron of a woman which seemed unnecessary because the apron and her dress were both filthy. We've had much communication since then on what an apron is really for. It seems that I might have been mistaken that an apron was to keep a woman's dress clean. We put it all together this way.

I remember a woman who wore an old checked apron when I was a boy. Actually, her apron was just another garment, but both full and wide. It filled its humble mission and a million more beside. It was made of six cent gingham, and it was neither fine nor grand. It was just a plain and simple pattern fashioned by an old and boney hand.

Now her apron had a little crossed stitch along the bottom row. It had two long strings that tied behind and looked somewhat like a bow. It didn't have any lace ruffles, just kinda hung like it was at play. But, its simple homely usefulness strikes a chord for that day.

Now, it was used to shoo the chickens, to dust, to shoo the flies. It was used to wipe the grimy tears from streaming children's eyes. It was used to fill the wood box with chips, cobs and twigs. And heck, that apron was used to tote the greens from the garden to the pigs.

This apron was used to carry home the eggs that an old hen had hidden, and it was used to snatch hot kettles then no pot holder was at hand. Why, it even tightened the fruit jars when things were being canned.

Why, this old apron was used to gather garden stuff and peaches from the hill. And many a mess of greens did this woman's apron fill. It shielded her hands from the wind beneath it's sheltering fold. And I've seen tiny little bare feet warming there on mornings that were so cold.

After thinking about it, this was a queenly garment, and this woman was really a queen. You folks have brought the memory back, and since then I've never seen a robe that was really as bright and fair. This old woman lay in her casket, and that old checked apron was what she had to wear.

FOOTNOTE: During the summer of 1934, Mrs. Willie Mae Frady was buried with her checked apron on. Her daughters insisted because she didn't look natural without it.

Flowers To The Living

We've had many characters here in Pickens County over the years worth writing about, but I have a favorite man I talk about a lot, mostly because everything I know about him is firsthand. I don't have to ask anyone anything. I know enough to fill a Sears, Roebuck catalog about Dr. J.S. Darnell of Jasper.

He was called "Doc" by everybody from the time they were old enough to talk until they were too old to talk. Doc was a pharmacist and owned and operated a drugstore in Jasper from about 1932 until about 1952. During these 20 years, his drugstore was the hangout for everybody, both old and young. Doc liked it this way, and you would often see him carrying on a conversation with a twelve-year-old boy just as seriously as he would any adult.

In the summer, both doors to the store remained wide open from 6:30 a.m. until 9 or 9:30 p.m. The latter depended largely on whether Doc was tired of talking or not.

There were two revolving-blade ceiling fans in the front and one at the back of the store. Neither did much cooling, but they did keep the flies run out of the store.

On the right as you entered was a pink marble soda fountain and three white marble-top tables down the center of the store, four wire drugstore chairs each. In the center of the tables were glass jars that kept the straws. Sometimes, two straws were used for one nickel drink by a couple of kids, but Doc didn't mind. He liked everybody.

This was during the Great Depression, and no one, no matter what his background was, was ever turned down for credit at Doc's drugstore.

He and I were sitting in the store one night when this man who everybody knew to be about as sorry as they come entered the store. He had three prescriptions and asked Doc if he would fill them and "set it down to him."

Doc looked at them, then he looked over his glasses at the man and said, "I'm going to fill the prescriptions because your folks need the medicine, but I'm not going to waste my time by writing it down." He filled them, and the man took the three bottles of medicine and left.

Nobody—and I mean *nobody*—was ever turned down in Dr. J.S. Darnell's drugstore for medicine just because they didn't have any money. He never sent statements. He always said people knew what they owed him; and if they wanted to pay him, they would, without spending three more cents postage mailing out bills. However, if he saw someone spending some money that maybe they shouldn't, and if they owed Doc a bill, the man would be called off in private, and Doc would tell him, "Say! If you have a little extra money, I could use some on your account."

Darnell often loaned people a little money to help them out of a tight spot. Some of it he got back, and some he didn't, but he never charged any interest to anyone.

There are many stories about this man that I would relate if I had the space. Doc had a cigar in his mouth all the time. It was lit part of the time, but most of the time it wasn't. He would use a carton of penny matches a day on one cigar, though.

Out front of the store were two loafers' benches that he had made and put there, one on each side of the doors. Quite often, you would see him sitting out there talking to someone, whether he be an older person or just a child.

Doc retired from the drugstore in 1952 and ran for county commissioner and was elected. Without going into details here, he made the best county commissioner that any county ever had.

I believe in "giving" folks their flowers while they are living. Dr. J.S. Darnell deserves them from thousands of people. As my old uncle W.B. Townsend, editor of the *Dahlonega Nugget*, used to say, "If you want to be remembered after death, write something worth reading or do something worth writing." Doc did this.

Waving Makes The Day Better

I've noticed lately that more and more of those little orange automatic hand-wavers are popping up in the windows of cars and trucks. There seems to be more of these in the city than in the country, and probably for good reason. It's not that people in the city are not friendly — it's probably that when you see several thousand people a day headed the other way, the idea of waving to each and every one of them starts to be a chore, so I guess this just might be the reason for so many automatic hand-wavers around the cities.

I'm still partial to more personalized greetings, though. A fellow here in town has a wave you can recognize from a half mile away. He's a big, bony guy, and his wave starts at about the center of the steering wheel and then sweeps back and forth across the top of the dash, going almost to the passenger-side vent window. When he waves at you, you know that you've been waved at.

There are all kinds of waves, but the casual wave is called for as you fog down a one-lane, dusty road in a pickup, meeting somebody fogging the other way in another pickup. The real pros usually just unwrap a couple of digits from the steering wheel and kind of hint an acknowledgement of the vehicle whizzing past a few inches away. This is always a tough wave for me in an old pickup that I sometimes drive, since it means relinquishing a bit more control than I have on that steering wheel that goes half way round at the least touch.

But there has always been something about having nearly everyone, complete strangers and all, toss you a wave. Getting a wave makes you feel good and accepted. Not getting one returned, by the same token, is mildly upsetting.

41

When we were kids, we used to really pour on the waving whenever a train came by, sometimes mimicking the motion of the engineer pulling down on the whistle cord, in hopes that he would give us a shot of the real thing. It was a great achievement if you coaxed a blast from the engineer. However, if the engineer saw us he usually obliged.

At least I thought he had until I eased onto the crossing over here in town one day and the engineer gave me both barrels. That's been several years ago—and somehow now I don't have any trouble stopping and looking before I ease up on that crossing.

It's easy to get out of the habit of waving and speaking if you are in the city very often, so I just don't try. I walk down Peachtree whenever I'm in Atlanta and speak to everyone I meet. Sometimes they respond, sometimes they don't. Either way, if you meet this old white-headed hillbilly, you are going to get spoken to. It's a nice habit, I think.

You Been Hugged Today?

Quite a case is being made these days for hugging. I like hugging. I like to be hugged occasionally by a young girl. (Good-looking in this case is irrelevant.) Almost everything becomes irrelevant when you get my age.

Virginia Satir, according to Bob Getz, (he's not the Getz that Getz them) is a social scientist who is thumping tubs on behalf of hugging. Who but a social scientist would have nothing better to do than run (amok?) around the country pointing out the obvious while bleating funny numbers that she passes off as legitimate full-fledged statistics?

Virginia Satir claims that four hugs a day are necessary for survival, eight for "maintenance" and 12 for growth. How she arrived at those figures, I don't know, and Mr. Getz says he doesn't either. I suppose, though, that she meant well, however she did it, but look at is this way. Wouldn't one hug from your son or daughter be worth 20 from your mother-in-law? And wouldn't one good hug from, say, Katie Lungsford, (she's here in the office) be worth more or do you more good than a thousand hugs from your loving Aunt Louella?

Then there is the other thing. Somehow I have the feeling that the hug quota or whatever you call it might vary from area to area, depending on community standards. That is, I would guess that there are some people who think that any more than three hugs, even between consenting adults, constitutes lewd and lascivious behavior. And if they ever saw a couple sharing 12 hugs for "growth," they'd probably report the man to the cops for sexual assault.

Virginia Satir says, "Our pores are messages of love." Lord have mercy on us all if hugging really catches on as an emotional necessity. For instance, not everybody has someone to hug or be hugged by, you know. So would people like that, desperate for some emotional maintenance, take to the streets and go on a hugging spree? Sprees?

Might a new breed of pervert emerge? Huggers? In crowds in broad daylight they could strike . . . Headlines: "The Peachtree Hugger" struck Thursday for the 90th time in the last 90 days when he leaped out into the crowd and hugged the 40-year-old lady returning to her work.

She might say, "Heck, I feel all cheered up about it. It wasn't so bad at all."

Opinions about the masked hugger vary. A local psychologist, Ralph C. Cussiun, who asked that his name be used if he were quoted in the paper, said, "Clinically speaking, I would have to say the Hugger is some kind of nut." But another psychiatrist, Julie Christleberry, said, "Actually, I think what this city needs are a few more huggers like that. I haven't been hugged since my divorce three years ago . . . ."

Who knows? Places called Hug Houses, where you might go and buy hugs, could even open up and flourish . . . . Four hugs for $5, eight for $9.50, something like that. Of course, if Hug Houses and Mad Huggers never become a reality, people desperately in need of hugs will always have somewhere to turn . . . . They can become TV game-show hosts.

Spread Jam And Roses Now

I got up the other morning and noticed in the obituary column of *The Atlanta Constitution* that an old army buddy had died. I hadn't heard from him in years, so I decided to drive the 100 miles to his funeral.

As I drove through the mountains along the crooked roads, my mind drifted back to a newspaper story about a soldier who refused to go to Washington for President Truman to pin a medal on him. It was the highest honor bestowed on a military person for "above and beyond the call of duty," or something along these lines. A hundred-dollar monthly check for life went along with the award.

The soldier called the $100 for life "socialism" and said that he didn't need a damn medal around the house to remind himself that he had killed his fellowmen just so he could survive.

I arrived at the funeral home in the small town shortly before the services were to begin. A large crowd was standing in the yard, and the home was overflowing with people. I recognized the deceased brother, whom I once met, and went up to him and told him who I was. He introduced me to the pallbearers, the president of the local bank, the mayor of the town, the local doctor and other "up-town folks."

My deceased friend's wife and two daughters spoke to me and seemed to be taking his death mighty hard. One of the daughters was leading a handsome five-year-old boy by the hand.

I walked on down to the cemetery where I was taken back by so many flowers. I have never seen as many flowers at a funeral in my whole life. The crowd came on shortly, but as soon as the undertaker placed the flag in the lap of my old army buddy's wife, I slipped away unnoticed.

I stopped at a small cafe for a cup of coffee before starting my journey home. Three seedy looking men were sitting in a booth. In true small town style one of the men asked if I were related to the deceased. "No," I answered, "just a friend of long ago."

The story began to unfold. My late friend had become an alcoholic and was found dead in the shack where he lived alone at the edge of town. His wife and children left him many years before, moving to another town. Today would be the first time the family had seen him in years. "He often talked about his grandson," said one of the men, "but he never got to see him."

"He didn't know the bank president," said the other, "and the only time that he ever saw the mayor was when he put him to work on the streets to pay off a fine."

"Nobody would help him," declared the first guy. "We were the only friends he had and weren't wanted at the funeral because we drank with him." The woman at the cash register nodded her head in agreement with what the men were saying. I paid her and hurried on outside where I got sick in the street.

I drove the lonely 100 miles home thinking these lines all the way, "When I quit this mortal shore, and mosey around this earth no more. Don't weep, don't sigh, don't sob; I may have struck a better job.

"Don't go and buy a large bouquet, for which you'll find it hard to pay. Don't mope around and feel all blue. I may be better off than you. Don't tell the folks I was a saint, or any old thing that I ain't. If you have jam like that to spread, please hand it out before I'm dead.

"If you have roses, bless my soul. Just pin one in my button hole while I'm alive and well today. Don't wait until I've gone away."

Fifth Grade Visit Fun

Reba Bell lives at Woodstock in Cherokee County, but she teaches the fifth grade at Cass Elementary School in Bartow County. Mrs. Bell called me one night and asked me to speak to her pupils.

I accepted and thought I would throw in a little extra, so I took Jack Carter, the oldest son of President Carter, with me. Of course the Secret Service men had to go along with us and that turned out to be a mistake — for Jack and me. The fifth graders, all in the 10-year-old group, were awed by seeing the men from the Treasury Department, one of whom had even served President Ford.

As a rule, these men stay in the background, never taking part in our conversation, and they try to appear as inconspicuous as possible. The radios they carry on their hips keep them in touch with all Secret Service departments in the area, where Atlanta is the main backup. Naturally, the kids were excited by all of this, but the agents drew the line when the kids asked to see their guns.

While there, I told the kids the Lewis Grizzard story about clean underwear. Lewis once said, "I suppose every mother asks her son if he has on clean underwear when he leaves the house."

"Why, Mama," Lewis quizzed one day, "do you always want to know if I have on clean underwear when I leave the house?"

"You might have a wreck," his mother replied.

And then ole Lewis said he dreamed one night about having a wreck. He was lying on the ground with blood all around when one of the doctors remarked, "Ole Lewis sure has got clean underwear."

When the principal of the school walked us down to Mrs. Bell's room, a football field away, he told us what a dedicated teacher she is. I was expecting to see one of those old maids who had been teaching for about one hundred years, but when we got to the classroom, the pretty young teacher I saw looked like one of the students.

My shoes, I thought, are older than she is.

I soon learned, though, why she is such a good teacher. Her students absolutely adored her and kids have got to love their teacher if they learn anything. We all know that.

I had a crush on all but one of my grammar school teachers. Ah, that one was one of those high-top-shoes characters with a wad of hair pinned up behind her head. I didn't learn a dern thing that year either. As you can see at times, that was the year when I was supposed to learn to spell.

Jack told the children about the White House. He emphasized that the president was just like any other person and he wanted them to know that every single one of them had the same chance of becoming president of the United States. Fifteen minutes later, he wanted to know if they had any questions. They all turned toward the Secret Service men and asked their questions.

A little black boy told me that his name was Carter and then a little white boy seated behind him said his name was Carter too. Jack, who had his back to us when I told him about the two little Carters remarked, "Hey, they may be kin to me."

And then he turned around to greet them. I kinda grinned, but the joke was on me as he gave the black Carter a big bear hug and then the white one a bear hug too. He called both of them "Cuzzins."

I wasn't expecting much attention, never do when I carry the president's boy along, but I nearly cried this morning when I got a whole bunch of letters in a brown envelope from the kids at the school. They told me they loved me and asked me back. And you can bet I will.

Visit some fifth graders some time. They may not get anything out of it, but you will.

Full Of Yellow Streaks

George Washington Towns was governor of Georgia. Zack Taylor was president of the United States, and Millard Fillmore was vice president. "The Virginia Reel" was the popular music and dance of the day. Wagons and horses were the transportation, but most folks walked wherever they went.

The time was 1849, the place Dahlonega, Georgia. William Benjamin Franklin Townsend would later own and publish *The Dahlonega Nugget*, and it was he who passed this story down to his nephew, namely me.

The gold had begun to peter out in Lumpkin County and the miners were talking excitedly about California. Matt Stephenson, the government assayer, was making every attempt to keep them from going. Stephenson, an educated man, pointed at the mountains declaring that there was still plenty of gold in the mountains around Dahlonega. Mark Twain later turned Mr. Stephenson's declaration into, "thar's gold in them thar hills." This might have been the first time a newspaper misquoted someone intentionally.

The reports that the assayer had been giving the prospectors for the last few days were beginning to make them suspicious. Matt Stephenson would say "nope" to the ore that was brought in, but always added, "There's evidence that there may be a rich vein somewhere in this vicinity." The miners finally concluded that the government assayer was tempting them just so they would stay on; after all, the assayer would be out of a job if all the miners left for California.

The men met one afternoon at the saloon next to the blacksmith shop. They would be leaving for the West the next morning and were doing a little celebrating. Matt Stephenson walked in and made one last stab at keeping the prospectors in Dahlonega. "There is plenty of rich lodes around here," he told them. The men told him to get lost, that their minds were made up.

The miners were getting very drunk when an idea struck one of them. The plan was to take some ore that they knew to be "wuthless" down to the assayer's office and if he said "there is a rich lode nearby," they would run him out of town.

The prospectors were looking around for some worthless rocks when someone spied the grindstone by the blacksmith shop. There wasn't anyone around so they hammered the axe sharpener into small pieces. Placing the contents in a bag, three men marched down to the assay office.

Mr. Stephenson was pleased at the new sudden interest, so he took great pains in testing the chunks. Then he exclaimed excitedly that the samples were of the highest grade of gold. "There is probably a rich lode somewhere near, too," he added.

The miners laughed at first, then they dragged the government assayer out of his office, and pushed him roughly down towards the saloon. The men guffahed and one suggested tar and feathers. A Mr. Parks threw down on the miners with a pistol and told Matt to leave, which he did mighty pronto.

Matt came out of hiding the next morning. The town was quiet. All the men had left early for their trip to the Promised Land of the west.

A couple of days later the blacksmith known only as a Mr. Rice came into the assay office. He showed Stephenson a couple of placer nuggets that he found out on the Chesatee River banks. The blacksmith had been over to Wahoo to visit a sick sister for the past few days, and when he returned his grindstone had been stolen.

He went out to the same place where he had gotten the sandstone for the missing grindstone. The blacksmith stuck his shovel in the same hole as before and the two nuggets appeared. Not only that, but the shovel full of sandstone was full of tiny yellow streaks.

Apples In The Mountains

It's apple pickin' time in the north Georgia mountains and will remain so until frost. The mountains are taking on a lazy look, and some of the leaves, turning brown prematurely, are falling off the trees. This is due to rain being scarce as .400 hitters this summer.

There was a time in these mountains when there would be fields of cotton this time of year—not large fields like you have in south Georgia, but big enough to look like a blanket of snow. But now, apples—that's the money crop up here these days.

Red ones and golden ones, and there are still some green ones. Apple trees cover the hillsides in every direction, and it's fun to watch the apples being picked off the trees. Sometimes the pickers will break out into an old spiritual just like in the old days in the cotton fields. "Life's evening sun is sinking low/A few more days and I must go."

The writers of Genesis did not name the fruit which Eve handed to Adam, yet the apple has carried the blame for this for centuries. Preachers have preached it, Sunday school teachers have taught it, and it's been handed down that it was the "pore ole" apple that caused all the trouble in the Garden of Eden.

According to *The Reader's Digest*, first there were tiny crab-apples by the mountain lakes of the Alps in Europe. Prehistoric people picked and cut and dried these inch-wide fruits, then buried them for the winter. Then, European crabapple trees were cross-bred with Asian crabapples, which produced the large modern apple. Englishmen leaving for the New World in the 1620's brought the apple seeds with them.

There are 1500 varieties of apples grown in the United States, but the mountains of north Georgia grow mostly Red Delicious, Golden Delicious, Rome Beauties, Winesap, Yates and Detroit Reds.

When I was a boy there was a June apple tree down in the branch bottom. This is the first apple to get ripe in the mountains. It's not much for size, about as big as a silver dollar, but this little apple was sweet and delicious to children who welcomed fresh fruit after a hard winter. I spent hours in this tree eating apples and reading Zane Grey as he brought my hero home safely. And, when Tom Swift invented something new, the apple tasted that much for the better.

 ## Why Jed Shot His $12,000 Bull

Jed McFarland lives pretty close to the Georgia line at the foot of a long range of mountains in east Tennessee. Jed is "well off" as they say up here when you mean someone is wealthy. There has always been a lot of talk that he made his money in whiskey, but nobody seems to give a hoot, including Jed.

Mack, as some call him, runs three hundred head of cattle in the greenest pasture you ever saw. The whiteface make a pretty picture grazing in the meadows with the huge white house on a small hill in the background, and the rippling of the creek is honey to one's ears.

I paid Jed a visit the other day and found him sitting in his rocker on the wrap-around porch overlooking his pastures and timberland. He invited me to lunch with the promise that they were going to have the highest-priced steak that money could buy. Minnie, his wife, is a good cook. I once spent the night there and we had crisp fried streak-of-lean and fried roast-neers for breakfast. This was topped off with sliced fried sweet potatoes, syrup and butter and hot biscuits. It was the best breakfast I ever ate with the best coffee that I ever tasted.

Jed had driven his new Buick down to the gate at the pasture, drove a few feet inside before parking his car and closing the gate. While he was walking out among the herd his prize bull looked at himself on the door of the car, then he trotted off about twenty feet, pawed a couple of times with his right front hoof and charged the reflection in the car door. Before Jed could do anything about it the bull went to the other side and did the same thing making the dash on the car look like it had been rolled over with a bulldozer. Mack was so mad that he took his rifle off the floorboard in the back seat and shot the animal. He had paid $12,000 for that thoroughbred.

What's more the insurance adjuster didn't want to do anything about the car, because he said it wasn't an accident. The bull meant to do it. The insurance man made the mistake that a lot of city folks make. He thought that Jed was "behind the door when the brains were passed out," just because he lives in the mountains. The insurance company paid off later.

Now, you might wonder about Jed being mad enough about his new Buick being totalled by the bull to shoot him. He has a thing about cars. He loves automobiles and has all kinds of literature and pictures of them from a Stanley Steamer and on up to the present-day cars. Many years ago Jed did a little shade-tree mechanicking. A big oak stood in his yard with a huge limb that always had a heavy chain across it. There was usually a car hoisted up by the front end, and you usually found Jed under it.

Just to show you how that insurance man was fooled, old Jed had books that told us where the word automobile came from. A French word meaning "self-movable." The book also informed us that the idea of self-propelled vehicles was first written about eight hundred B. C. in Homer's *Iliad* which mentions twenty marvelous three-wheeled vehicles that were self-moved.

McFarland also has a diary on cars that his family has owned which is very interesting and complete with pictures. Jed's father had a Studebaker that was made in 1911 which he learned to drive in 1920 when he was twelve years old. Then his Pa owned about every car that came along, and at the age of thirteen Jed, with his own money, bought a Packard that was built in 1912. The back seat was removed for the purpose of transporting non-tax-paid whiskey. In 1925 he bought a brand new Chrysler, one of the first built. "Went all the way to Detroit for it, me and Paw," he said, and on the way back "stayed the night in one of them tourist courts that was springing up along the highways."

Jed has pictures and information on about every automobile made. All sorts of Model "T's" from 1914 to the "A" Models in 1927. Pictures of the 1914 cars adorn the walls of his house. Jackson, Hupmobile, Hudson, Mitchell, Maxwell, Overland, and Franklin, but the Model "T," always black, outsold them all, according to Jed's history of old cars.

There is a 1900 Dodge, Chevrolet, and Oldsmobile on his wall, and according to him, this was the first year they made them. He recalled a song of the twenties, "Come Away With Me Lucille, in My Merry Oldsmobile." The 1920 Cadillac and Essex were sporty, but there were others too — the Ford with a rumble seat in 1928-1929, the first V8 Ford of 1932, the Whippet and many others.

Jed says some folks wrote all over their cars in the twenties and thirties like "I'm From Texas, You Can't Steer Me," and so on. He believes this is where the bumper sticker idea started, and the "T" shirt monograms came from the college kids' raincoats of the twenties and thirties.

Very interesting fellow, Jed McFarland, but you would have to know him and his love for cars to understand why he shot that $12,000 bull. Anyway, the steak was pretty good, but didn't taste any better than any other steak that I've eaten . . . especially that down at "Mabel's Bar and Grille."

You Must Remember This...

Days Gone By

Every second car on the road was a Ford in 1920. It now is a closed-in sedan if you prefer, with window shades and a side-mounted spare tire. The luxury Cadilac added a searchlight. The Essex and Apperson are now on the road. The expressions now new to the language are "all wet," "applesauce," "baloney," "banana oil," "belly laugh," "bump off," "carry a torch," "fall guy," "gate crasher," and "sex appeal." The song *Margie* was sung and revived as a popular song in the thirties.

Bobby Jones caused shock and furor in 1921 when he walked off the course and quit the match at the British Open. Bill Tilden again won the tennis singles championships. The Miss America contest was started in Atlantic City. "I'm Just Wild About Harry," "Ain't We Got Fun," and "Wabash Blues" are favorites.

The songs "My Buddie," "Toot, Toot Tootsie," "Way Down Yonder in New Orleans" in 1922. Paul Whiteman was King of Jazz. The roaring twenties are now here.

In 1923 Bobby Jones wins his first U.S. Open. The Charleston is the dance and a song of the same name became a hit. "Yes, We Have No Bananas," "Barney Google," "I Cried for You," "That Old Gang of Mine" were "ins" also.

Cars had their windshield wipers in 1923. While in 1924, Ford got it's first self-starter, yet men still went around with broken arms because they still made a Ford without the starter which sold for $290.

In 1925 Fords had been in black only but now offered a green and maroon. Popular now on the road are the Apperson, Buick, Franklin, Haynes, Locomobile, Oldsmobile, Overland, Auburn, Cord, Cunningham, Stutz, Cadillac V12 and V16, Packard, and Lincoln. Tourist Courts are now along the highways and so are Burma Shave signs.

Here comes a nifty little car in 1926, the Overland Whippet, with four-wheel brakes. It later became the Willis Whippet. Airlines are now spreading as Sports is the King of the twenties. The Model A Ford came on in 1927 as there are now twenty-three million cars on the road. Yes, "Charlie Somebody," I did miss "Stardust" and "Tip Toe Through the Tulips," which were popular in 1929, so I think it's time that we quit reminiscing. I hope everybody has had as much fun reading it as I have had researching it.

To answer one more, the Studebaker Company made two horse wagons and buggies until 1911. The company converted to making automobiles at this time.

1927: Long-Count Prize Fight

Mrs. Jane Rausch, age 82, writes that she has been a sports fan all of her life and the 70,000 fans at the Rose Bowl on January 1, 1929 was not the largest crowd to ever attend a sporting event in America. She says that 105,000 people were at the second Dempsey-Tunney fight in Chicago, September 22, 1927.

Mrs. Jane is correct, of course, and while I meant that the 70,000 at the Rose Bowl was the largest crowd to ever see a football game, the mistake is mine. She goes farther by saying that this championship bout should be the number one news item over the past 60 years.

I suppose this would depend largely on which sport a person likes the best, but there are many sporting events which take their place in somebody's mind. I know that Mark is not going to let me turn this page into a sports page, but going back to the year of 1927, Babe Ruth hit 60 home runs for the Yankees, talking pictures with Al Jolson in "The Jazz Singer" made their debut and Lindbergh made his solo flight across the Atlantic.

This was the time when "Ol' Man River," "Yes Sir, That's My Baby," "Five Foot Two, Eyes of Blue," and "Show Me the Way to Go Home" were popular songs. Jim Richards from Jasper was at the fight in Soldiers Field, Chicago. For many years someone would bring up the subject of the "long count" and that they thought Dempsey really won the match. Jim would reply, "That's what y'all think that didn't see the fight."

Tunney had won the first fight with Dempsey on points in the 10-rounder staged at Philadelphia in the rain the year before. The first fight drew a million-dollar gate and the second went to two and one-half million. Tunney outboxed Dempsey for seven rounds and was ahead on points when Dempsey caught him with a left hook, flooring the champ. Dempsey stood over Tunney and refused to go to a neutral corner as was the rule before the ref was to begin counting. Tunney started to get up but his manager yelled for him to stay down. Four seconds lapsed before Dempsey went to the neutral corner and the referee started his count. There was a reason for this and to understand we will have to go back to

1923. That was the year the "The Four Horsemen" of Notre Dame ran wild, and this was the year that Bobby Jones won his first U.S. Open. This was the year that "Charleston," "That Old Gang of Mine," and "Toot, Toot, Tootsie" were the top songs.

It was at the Polo Grounds in New York, on September 14, that Jack Dempsey met Luis Firpo from Argentina, and labeled "The Wild Bull of the Pampas." Firpo smashed Dempsey with a right at the beginning of the first round, and later blasted him out of the ring and into the laps of the press. The men helped Dempsey back into the ring which was against the rules. Firpo should have been declared the winner, but instead Dempsey knocked Firpo down. This was repeated seven times and after each knockdown Dempsey, instead of going to a neutral corner, would slug Firpo as he got up. After one knockdown Dempsey stepped over Firpo to get a better shot at him as he got up. Dempsey slugged Firpo as hard as he could while he was on his knees. Nobody ever knew why the referee permitted all this, but the rumor was that he was afraid of the gamblers who had bet on Dempsey.

This was the reason for the long count. Tunney, having seen the Firpo match and other Dempsey fights, didn't want Dempsey to hit him as he got to his feet. After the notorious long count Tunney knocked Dempsey down in the ninth and tenth rounds. Jim Richards told us that Dempsey's face looked like he had been stung by ten thousand hornets, one eye was closed and he was bloody as a stuck hog. "Tunney," according to Richards, "looked as fresh as a daisy." Tunney was awarded the decision. Dempsey, afraid of going blind, refused another rematch.

So, it just depends on how you look at things that we think are more important than others. Tunney retired from the ring undefeated soon afterward in 1928. During this same year Ty Cobb also retired from baseball with a lifetime average of .323, and Sonja Heinie and Johnny Weismuller began their careers at the Olympics. "Button Up Your Overcoat," "You're the Cream in My Coffee," "I Can't Give You Anything But Love," "Lover Come Back," and "Sweet Sue," were now popular. Crossword puzzles were a craze and playing bridge was a madness. Black Bottom was added to The Charleston and The Shimmey as popular dances. Bill Robinson won first place in buck dancing, while Fred Astaire came in second.

Remembering The Wrong Way Run

The letter from a member of the Associated Press asked me to send a list of what I thought were the top 10 stories that happened during my lifetime. Oddly enough, the top story in my opinion happened 52 years ago and involved Georgia Tech. But, really, should any sports stories be included in the top 10?

I think so, because on New Year's Day the story of Roy Riegals' wrong-way run in the Rose Bowl on Jan. 1, 1929, is always mentioned. It's mentioned by those who remember and by the young folks who have either read or heard about it. It's only fitting that we mention here that during this same year Connie Mack, manager of the Philadelphia Athletics baseball team, was awarded the $10,000 Edward Bok prize, an award previously given to scientists, philanthropists and the like.

These were the days where there were only 557 radio stations in the nation. These were the days when "Tip Toe Through the Tulips," "Three Little Words," "My Blue Heaven" and "Walking My Baby Back Home" were the hit songs. These were the days of the flapper with rolled stockings, long cigarette holder, short skirt and boyish bob.

In Pasadena, Calif., Georgia Tech defeated the Golden Bears of California in the Rose Bowl, 8-7. The 70,000 fans were the largest crowd to ever attend a sports event. The fans almost went crazy in the second quarter when Roy Riegals of California, playing center, snatched up a Tech fumble and started toward the Georgia Tech goal. Tech men jumped up in front of him and, eluding them, Riegals cut back across the field. He turned again to get away from the Tech tacklers and in so doing became confused and started toward his own goal 60 yards away. As he ran down the sideline, both California and Tech players stood amazed in their tracks. The yelling fans were so astonished that they became so quiet that you could hear Riegals breathing as he ran.

Benny Lom, halfback for the University of California, sensed the situation almost immediately and took off after Riegals, who only put on more speed as he heard the thundering hoofs behind him. Finally, Lom grabbed hold of his mate at the California three-yard line and turned him around. Lom started back up the field running interference for Riegals but a wave of Georgia Tech tacklers hit Riegals, knocking him back to the one-yard line.

California went into a punt formation but Riegals at center was nervous and so was Lom who was to kick the ball. As the ball snapped, Maree, the Georgia Tech tackle, stormed through and blocked the punt. The ball touched Breckenridge, California's quarterback, and rolled into the end zone. A safety was ruled by the referee, making the score Tech 2, California 0.

Tech's touchdown came in the third quarter. Missing the extra point made the score Tech 8, California 0. California's touchdown came in the final minutes of the game. The extra point was good and the final score was 8-7. The folks in Atlanta paraded up and down Peachtree Street all night long and on up into the next day singing "Happy Days Are Here Again."

Will Poole, of this small town of Jasper, was a Georgia Tech graduate and was at the game.

He told this story for many years around Doc Darnell's drug store. Mountain people who had never seen a football game enjoyed hearing about this event over and over. It has been said that Poole attracted a bigger crowd when he started telling about his trip to Pasadena than James Lenning did when he returned from the gold fields in 1849.

We come again to the New Year, the beginning of another era. We are now blessed with another handful of time which is precious at my age of 61. Were it not for the observance of a New Year, the passing of time might be monotonous and meaningless. We would watch the endless pattern of days and nights without fully realizing that time, like money, must be spent wisely or else it's wasted. That is why we need the New Year to remind us that time has been spent or wasted, and a little more valuable time is now ours to use or waste away.

So Happy New Year, everybody, and a very Happy New Year to you, Roy Riegals, wherever you are.

The Market Crash

Fifty years ago, in the year 1929, the stock market crash started a depression that rocked the world. The sudden drop in the market was on Oct. 29 and was labeled by the media as "Black Tuesday" . . . 95 percent of the wealth in America was now in the hands of 10 percent of the people.

The years started off with a boom with investors buying on margin, consumers bought on the installment plan. Chain stores and supermarkets boomed too. A&P now had more than 15,000 stores, J.C. Penny had 4,000.

The year 1929 will be remembered by those of us who witnessed it. It will also be remembered by those who have read about it, and those who have heard their parents talk about it.

Herbert Hoover was sworn in as President. Dr. Hardeman was governor of Georgia, and Richard B. Russell was speaker of the house of representatives. Folks were still singing "Sweet Sue," "Buttom Up Your Overcoat," "I Can't Give You Anything But Love, Baby," "Lover Come Back," and "There's A Rainbow Round My Shoulders." They were still dancing the Charleston and Shimmy, and a new dance, The Black Bottom, was added.

There were now 12 million radios in America and announcers began to be celebrities. H.V. Kaltenborn was a commentator, "There's Good News Tonight." And Kate Smith was the "Songbird of the South." "When The Moon Comes Over The Mountain" was Kate's theme. Amos and Andy went on and so did Rudy Valee, the "Vagabond Lover," and Red Arthur Godrey sang into a mike for the first time.

On Feb. 14, a group of Chicago gangsters, wearing police uniforms, gunned down seven rivals in a garage, in what became known as the Saint Valentine's Day Massacre.

Al Capone was the gangland boss of Chicago. 1,000 killings went by without a single conviction. A monthly magazine, *True Story*, was the hottest seller in the United States, selling 4 million copies each month.

Some new songs became hits, "Ain't Misbehaving," "Stardust," "Tip Toe Through The Tulips," "Singing In The Rain," "Happy Days Are Here Again," and "Sweethearts On Parade," while couples rode in rumble seats of autmobiles. The new safety glass in cars has now enclosed about 80 percent of all cars. Others still got out and put up the curtains when it looked like rain. The popular cars of the day were the A Model Ford, Chevrolet and Packard was the elegant vehicle.

Charles Lindbergh married Ann Morrow, daughter of the U.S. Ambassador to Mexico. Albert Fall, Secretary of the Interior under Harding, was sentenced to one year in prison and fined $100,000 for accepting a bribe in the Teapot Dome Scandal. Philadelphia awarded the $10,000 Edward W. Bok prize—an award previously given to scientists, philanthropists, and the like—to Connie Mack, manager of the Athletics baseball club.

Georgia Tech fans were thrilled back on Jan. 1, 1929, when Tech defeated the University of California in the Rose Bowl by a score of 8-7. The game was marked as Roy Riegals, center for the Golden Bears' "wrong way run." While fans all over Georgia celebrated, no one knew, of course, what was in store for the fall of 1929.

Oct. 29, Black Tuesday—$30 billion in paper money was wiped out in a single week. The stock of Union Cigar went from $115 to $2 in a single day, and the company's president jumped from the ledge of a hotel.

"In Wall Street, every wall is wet with tears." The market for consumer goods was gutted. It was a black time and would get blacker before the Great Depression which followed would end 12 or 15 years later.

Miniature golf was a craze with "little links" popping up all across America. The fad on college campuses was gold fish swallowing and women's hair started back from the "devil's boyish bobs" to longer styles and permanent waves. "Three Little Words" was now a popular song on the graphonolas, and so was "Walking My Baby Back Home," and "On The Sunny Side Of The Street."

Time marches on . . . .

The Depression Years

This year marks the anniversary of the stock market crash which rocked the world. The sudden drop in the market came on October 24, 1929 and came to be known as "Black Friday." Herbert Hoover had been President of the United States for only seven months, yet he would carry the blame for the depression that followed to his grave.

Bridge playing was a madness in '29, Philippe de Brassiere, a former wartime flying ace, designed a chest halter for women which still bears his name. This was the year that installment buying began on a large scale. Most of the cars were now closed and called "houses of prostitution" by a judge in Indiana.

On February 14th, a group of Chicago gangland killers wearing police uniforms gunned down seven rivals in a garage, in what became known as the Saint Valentine's Day Massacre. "True Story," a confessions magazine, came on the market while lipstick now was commonplace. Songs of the day were "Ain't Misbehaving," "Stardust," "Tip Toe Through the Tulips" and "Singing in the Rain."

In the year 1930, the airline stewardess came aboard the airlines which were now beginning to compete with railroads. The crazes now were miniture golf, backgammon, and on college campuses, goldfish swallowing. "I Got Rhythm," "Three Little Words," "Walking My Baby Back Home," and "On the Sunny Side of the Street" were the hit songs as the depression deepened.

Bootlegging and gangsterism reached a peak as Al Capone took over in Chicago. 1000 gangland killings went unsolved by the police. The country went wild for the Tarzan movies. Bobby Jones won golf's grand slam.

The "Star Spangled Banner" became our national anthem in 1931. Men wore baggy knickers while women's hats became popular. Al Capone was sentenced to 11 years for income tax evasion. "Legs Diamond," another gangster, was killed while he slept in New York. The Depression deepened as banks were closing all across the country. Thousands were now on the roads and hoboing freights. Knute Rockne, Notre Dame coach, was killed in a plane crash. "I Found a Million Dollar Baby in a Five and Ten Cent Store," and "Minnie the Moocher" wwere being sung or whistled by almost everyone.

Double features at the movies with bank nights became popular in 1932 as the Depression continued to get worse. 20 million people were now unemployed as the Veterans of World War I organized a bonus march on Washington. General Douglas McArthur attacked them with his troops, running the vets out of town.

Ford's new V-8 was an instant success and, with its quick take off, became the favorite getaway car for gangsters like Clyde Barrow and John Dillinger. Cotton is now five cents a pound, eggs six cents a dozen as farmers became desperate. It had become a myth that President Hoover did not accept his salary, but records indicate that he only lowered his pay by $2000 a year, to $73,000 a year.

Franklin D. Roosevelt was elected President, but all he had to do to win was stay alive. Lou Gehrig hit four home runs in one game. Jack Sharkey defeated Max Schmeling and the popular saying, "I yam what I yam," was brought out by Popeye.

1933 brought FDR's initial programs, unemployed boys were taken off the streets and hired for the CCC camps. AAA was to aid the farmer. Children are now going hungry in the United States. Soup lines were in cities with little relief. The TVA and PWA begins here. Fads were Jigsaw puzzles as people still sang the leftover music from the previous year, "Brother Can You Spare a Dime?", "I'm Getting Sentimental Over You," "Night and Day" and "Let's Have Another Cup of Coffee."

An attempt by Joseph Zangara to assassinate FDR in Miami failed, but the shot killed the mayor of Chicago, Anton Germak. Hoovervilles, shantytowns occupied vacant lots in cities and apple sellers were on street corners. The times are now critical, a million transients are on the road, 200,000 are children. Hungry children. The Chicago World's Fair opened featuring Sally Rand, a stripper. No jobs, very little money, yet people would sing and listen to "Smoke Gets in Your Eyes," "Stormy Weather," "Who's Afraid of the Big Bad Wolf" and "Easter Parade."

"I suppose that taking care of people runs against the grain — against the feeling that everyone ought to hustle for himself. But there comes a time when people can't hustle anymore." So said Dr. James Edward Townsend, who founded the old age pension which developed into social security. He went to jail for it. This is 1934. Shirley Temple became popular and the Dionne Quintuplets were born.

During 1934, sirloin steak was 23 cents a pound, milk ten cents a quart and potatoes were two cents a pound. Things are bad. Children are suffering from hunger and exposure, no medicine and no money, yet the songs of the day were "Blue Moon," "Stars Fell on Alabama," "All Through the Night," "On the Good Ship Lollipop."

The FBI rode high in 1934 when they killed John Dillinger, Pretty Boy Floyd, and Baby Face Nelson and Bonnie and Clyde were riddled with bullets in their stolen Ford V-8 after a reign of terror and murders.

Max Baer became world heavyweight champ, knocking out Max Schmeling. Young Joe Louis won his first fight. "Blue Moon" became number one on the Hit Parade. "Begin the Beguine" was second. "Cheek to Cheek" was moving up.

The Depression lasted 10 years. Ten long years and trying to describe it here will go for nothing. You have to live in one to believe it. Now in 1979 we are going through Inflation. I've been through both. Inflation or Depression. . .I'll take Inflation every time.

Gas Rationing And More Good Songs...

Gas rationing, tire rationing, Savings Bonds, Savings Stamps and aerosol sprays were introduced in 1941. The year's draft was now in full swing as the Andrews Sisters sang "This Is the Army, Mr. Jones." On December 7, the Japs bombed Pearl Harbor, killing 3,958 people. The U.S. declared war on Japan the following day. On December 11, Italy and Germany declared war on the U.S.

This year fans watched Joe Louis defend his title an unbelieveable seven times. He defeated Red Burman, Gus Forzaio, Abe Simon, Tony Musto, Buddy Baer, Billy Conn and Lou Nova. Joe Demaggio hit safely in fifty-six consecutive games. Lou Gehrig died.

Rita Hayworth was "The Love Goddess," while songs being sung were "Chattanooga Choo Choo," "Blues in the Night," "Jersey Bounce," "Green Eyes," and "I've Got It Bad and That Ain't Good."

In the year 1942, the WACS, the Waves and the Spars, all women's service organizations, were made fact. But do you recall "Deep in the Heart of Texas" or "Praise the Lord and Pass the Ammunition"? The Andrews Sisters made boys think of home with "Don't Sit Under the Apple Tree," while juke organs played "I've Got Spurs that Jingle Jangle Jingle," "That Old Black Magic" and "White Christmas."

It was a sad day in 1942 when Bataan and Corregidor fell to Japan. The Japs invaded about every dot in the Pacific Ocean.

Zoot Suiters hit the streets in the American cities in 1943, while the U.S. finally secured Guadalcanal in January after the most bitter hand-to-hand fighting of the Pacific. The British and American armies linked together and drove the Germans from North Africa. Leslie Howard was killed as his plane was shot down by the Germans. "Pistol Packing Mama," "Mairzy Doats," "Coming in on a Wing and a Prayer," "Do Nothing 'Til You Hear from Me," "Oh, What a Beautiful Morning," "Surrey with the Fringe on Top," and "As Time Goes by," from Humphrey Bogart's *Casablanca* all made it big. Now, if you want to come with me to 1944 when the German V-2 missile was about to destroy London. And, of course, you remember "Kilroy" coming on the scene and according to signs that rascal had been about everywhere.

Songs were "Rum and Coca-Cola," "Ac-cent-tchu-ate the Positive," "Don't Fence Me In," "Long Ago and Far Away," and "I'll Be Around." D-Day landing came on June 6, on Normandy Beach. FDR defeated Tom Dewey for his fourth term. Harry Truman was his Vice. Comic strips were a rage among troops. Meanwhile, back at the ranch, Bill Mauldin's weary GI Joes and Gerge Baker's Sad Sack drew laughs. "Kilroy Was Here" would become a legend.

1945. The war in Italy ended on April 29, and Germany surrendered on May 7. On April 12, less than a month from V-Day, President Roosevelt died at Warm Springs, Georgia. Truman was sworn in as President. An American B-29 built at Marietta, Georgia dropped the first atomic bomb on the city of Hiroshima on August 6, killing half the population. Three days later a second bomb was dropped on Nagasaki, killing another 40,000. Japan surrendered on August 14th with the formals taking place aboard the battleship Missouri on September 2.

The songs of 1945 were "Atchison, Topeka and the Santa Fe," "Personality," "Sentimental Journey," and "These Foolish Things" reappeared.

In 1946 we saw the introduction of Kaiser-Frazer cars, electric clothes driers, electric blankets and automatic transmissions. "No down payment" neighborhoods jumped up all across the nation.

California Republican Richard Nixon was elected to Congress, and so was John F. Kennedy of Massachusetts.

"Zip-a-Dee-Doo-Dah," "How Are Things in Glocca Morra?" and "There's No Business Like Show Business," were the favorite songs. Crew cuts for men were stylish.

Blacks were in major league baseball for the first time when Jackie Robinson joined the Brooklyn Dodgers in 1947. "Open the Door Richard" and "Tenderly" were the "in" songs. TV came to Atlanta with "Meet the Press" moving over from radio and "Howdy Doody" dug in for a long run.

1948 is when President Truman defeated Tom Dewey in an upset. The *New York Times* early morning papers headlines announced Dewey as the winner. Do you remember that 21-21 tie between Navy and Army's Doc Blanchard and Junior Davis? The rest of 1948 went to music. . ."Buttons and Bows," "It's So Peaceful in the Country," "On a Slow Boat to China," and "All I Want for Christmas is My Two Front Teeth," followed in 1950 with "Mule Train," "Baby It's Cold Outside," and "Rudolph the Red-Nosed Reindeer."

On To The Fifties

The fifties brought an avalanche of credit as the Diners Card and others were being used more by the middle income group. This type of credit had been reserved for the upper income group until this period and folks took advantage of it, not realizing that a flood of inflation was now beginning. President Truman attacked the six-cent candy bar as inflationary.

In 1950 war broke out between North and South Korea. Gen. MacArthur was named commander of the U.N. forces to battle the communist aggression. China threw one million troops in the war on the side of North Korea. Nobody missed them in China. The North Koreans were pushed back to the 38th Parallel. MacArthur wanted to follow and bomb China and was fired as Commander by President Truman.

Red fever broke out in the United States and Senator Joe McCarthy labeled about everybody in America a communist except himself. Folks stayed glued to television watching the McCarthy hearings. Songs of the day were "Music, Music, Music," "Tennessee Waltz," "Goodnight Irene" and "Chattanooga Shoe Shine Boy." Rita Hayworth married Prince Aly Khan, and Joe Louis tried a comeback but lost to Ezzard Charles.

1951 introduced more bank credit cards as inflation was growing. Power steering on Buicks and Chryslers and color TV were the majors of science.

The twenty-second amendment was passed limiting a President to two terms, and now Americans were watching the Kefauver's hearings on organized crime. Julius and Ethyl Rosenberg were sentenced to die for spying. They were executed in 1953 when Ike refused to commute their sentence. Penicillin and streptomycin were the wonder drugs, as the popular songs were "Shrimp Boats" and "On Top of Old Smoky." Joe Dimaggio retired from baseball. Paperbacks became best sellers.

In 1952 the first Holiday Inn opened in Memphis, Tenn., and listen to this: a potato shortage developed and a black market developed as price controls were still in effect. The hydrogen bomb was exploded in the Marshall Islands. Ike was elected over Adlai Stevenson. Richard Nixon became Vice-President. Rocky Marciano became heavyweight champ and "High Noon" was the favorite song, followed by "Wish You Were Here" and "I Saw Mommy Kissing Santa Claus."

1953 saw "Your Cheating Heart" as the most popular song followed by "How Much Is That Doggie in the Window?" 3-D movies came along and Scrabble, a 20-year-old game, finally caught on. The New York Yankees defeated the Brooklyn Dodgers to win five world championships in a row. Men looked silly with hairy legs and Bermuda shorts, making it look even worse when they put on knee socks. McCarthy was still investigating everybody for communism.

The Packard Motor Company folded in 1954. Racial segregation was declared unconstitutional in public schools while McCarthy's witch hunt continued. A recession hit America when former President Truman remarked, "Small wonder. Ike doesn't know how to buy an aspirin tablet for himself." The dance craze is the Cuban Mambo while songs are "Mister Sandman," "Three Coins in the Fountain," "Hey There" and "Shake, Rattle and Roll."

McDonald's opened their first hamburger restaurant in Illinois and the Ford Thunderbird was introduced in 1955. The movie "King of the Wild Frontier" set off a fad of coonskin caps while "Davy Crockett" was being sung by almost all youngsters and a heap of adults. "Sixteen Tons," "The Yellow Rose of Texas," and "Love is a Many Splendored Thing" were the favorites. Ed Sullivan featured Elvis Presley on his show but the camera only showed Presley from the waist up. Rock and Roll is now here, folks. "It Won't Last," said Lawrence Welk.

1956 was a slow year but the Salk vaccine proved effective against polio. The New York Yankee's Don Larsen pitched the first perfect game in a world series. The Dodgers were on the short end again. "Peyton Place" was the most talked about book while Elvis sang, "Jailhouse Rock." "Tammy" came up in the ratings, too, and so did "Love Me Tender," "Hound Dog," "Around the World in 80 Days" and "Standing On a Corner."

The Nash, Hudson and Packard automobiles were no more in 1957. Billy Graham comes on strong, packing in 92,000 at the Yankee Stadium in this year, too. Here come the "beatnics" with their own language which set off a movement that lowered standards of the world. Best song was "Kisses Sweeter Than Wine."

1958, automobile tail fins were in their glory. After 34 years in prison, Nathan Leopold of the Leopold-Loeb thrill murder was paroled. Leob had been killed many years before by another inmate. Sherman Adams, special asst. to President Eisenhower, was forced to resign in the face of a scandal for accepting bribes. "The Chipmunk Song" and "Tom Dooley" were the favorite songs and the cha-cha and rock were the dances.

The compact cars came on in 1959 and the food stamp program for the poor was introduced. The biggest fad since the yo-yo was introduced as the hoola hoop. Alaska and Hawaii were admitted to the Union. Television quiz shows came on strong, giving away large sums of money while radio had its payola scandal. "High Hopes" and "He's Got the Whole World in His Hands" were the disc jockey specials.

We saw the "twist" in 1960. John Kennedy defeated Richard Nixon by a hair for the Presidency in 1960. The "New Fontier" is now about to begin as folks sing, "My Home Town."

The Sixties Brought Missiles,
The Twist And Jimmy Carter

The younger group has asked us to do some highlights from the sixties. 1960 was the year that John Kennedy was elected President, Ernest Vandiver was in his second year as governor of Georgia. Women's heads doubled in size from the bouffant hairdo. Turtle neck sweaters were accepted in the place of ties for men in most places. Songs like "Never on Sunday," "The Twist," and "My Home Town" were popular.

Kennedy was inaugurated. "Viguh" and "Cuber" crept into the language. Jackie Gleason's TV show from Miami Beach was a hit in 1961. "Please Mr. Postman," "Love Makes the World Go Round," and "Calcutta" were popular songs.

1962 is the year that wigs arrived, and John Glenn became the first American to orbit the earth. The "Cuber" crisis arose when Russian missile buildup was discovered there by U.S. Intelligence. Mrs. Eleanor Roosevelt died, and President Kennedy dispatched troops to Mississippi to enter James Merideth, a black, in college. Songs were "Rambling Rose," "Days of Wine and Roses," "Go Away Little Girl," and "You Are My Sunshine" was revived. Carl Sanders defeated former Governor Marvin Griffin for governor of Georgia in a knock down, drag out affair.

In 1963 "The Beverly Hillbillies," a TV show, was called ignorant and given two months, and then promptly rose to the top of the ratings. President Kennedy was assassinated. Lyndon Johnson was sworn in as President. Campus riots are raging. A very bad year as the popular songs were "If I Had a Hammer" and "Louie, Louie."

The 24th Amendment ended the poll tax for voters in 1964. The Beatles took the U.S. by storm as they appeared first on Ed Sullivan's show. Discotheques became the place, and Go-Go dancers were the thing. Songs like "Hello Dolly," "Amen," "Downtown," "Going Out of My Head," and "I Want to Hold Your Hand" were the favorites of disc jockeys. Campus riots continued protesting the Viet Nam War which had by now become a catastrophe. President Johnson was elected over Barry Goldwater.

1965 was the year of the miniskirts. Civil riots, marches, and campus disturbances are now raging. Songs like "What the World

73

Needs Now," "Help," "Mr. Tambourine Man," and "Yesterday" were popular. Daytime game shows, "Flipper," and "The King Family" were popular TV shows. Here come more beatniks, more unrest in the country and rock shows brought some weirdos such as the Mamas and the Papas, the Hollies and Neil Diamond, and 1966 with "These Boots Are Made for Walking," "Yellow Submarine," "Georgy Girl" and "Somewhere My Love." Jimmy Carter ran for governor of Georgia and lost to Lester Maddox.

1967 brought the hippies and paper dresses. The war in Vietnam was getting worse as U.S. bombers attacked Hanoi. Shirley Temple Black failed in a try for Congress as a Republican. "Valley of the Dolls" set a record for paperbacks. Songs "Feeling Groovy," "Michelle," "By the Time I Get to Phoenix," "Cabaret," "Sunrise Sunset," "Ode to Billy Joe" and "San Francisco" were in.

Campus riots made headlines in 1968 as students protested the Vietnam War. Protests, marches and sit-ins were on fire as the year rolled on. Nixon defeated Hubert Humphrey for President. Spiro Agnew was his Vice who later had to resign as a result of a financial scandal. Plane hijackings were on the move with Cuba the main destination. Songs, "Hey Jude," "Those Were the Days," "Little Green Apples" and "Hold Me Tight" were the most popular. Guitar pieces, "Galveston" and "Wichita Lineman," were high on the list of disc jockeys.

1969 introduced disposable diapers. Ouija boards and occult groups were on the increase. Man walked on the moon while 600 million watched on TV. Mary Jo Kopechne drowned. Senator Kennedy pleaded guilty to leaving the scene of a fatal accident and received a two month suspended sentence. The comical New York Mets won the World Series, defeating Baltimore four games to one. Rod Laver took the Men's Tennis titles at Wimbleton. Songs "Hurry on Down," "Raindrops Keep Falling on My Head," "Let the Sunshine In," "I'll Never Fall in Love Again," "Yesterday When I Was Young," "My Cup Runneth Over," and "Everybody's Talking" were the hits.

1970, Jimmy Carter was elected governor of Georgia, defeating former Governor Carl Sanders. All the polls had picked Sanders the winner. Carter would go on to be elected President of the United States, the first Georgian to ever hold this office. . . .Country and Western music is now rolling, and so is gospel music, with gospel groups entering the big money market for the first time.

There's Hope For The 80's

So far, the eighties haven't been as wacky as the seventies, and for everybody's sake I hope they never are. Israel and Egypt made peace in the seventies, George Willig climbed the World Trade Center in New York City. (Now he's on the circuit tour, a true seventies' hero.) A student at St. Mary's University in San Antonio swallowed two hundred ten goldfish to claim a world record. A man in California spent twenty-two days lying on a cot and got into Guiness. The song of the year in 1976 was "Send in the Clowns."

Wacky? Henry Kissenger won a peace prize in 1973 for ending a war that didn't end until 1975. But the seventies was a decade that started with *Love Story*, and ended in Jonestown. The suicide of the seventies was really committed by Chris Chubbuck, a thirty year old Sarasota, Florida, talk show hostess who appeared before her viewers one morning and shot herself in the head.

Back in 1969 Neil stepped onto the moon. Teddy drove off a bridge and Sesame Street made its television debut. The sixties were over. The seventies had to be better, but were they? D. B. Cooper dropped out of a plane with two hundred thousand dollars in 1971 and disappeared. John Dean was made the villain for speaking up, Gordon Liddy became a martyr for keeping his mouth shut. *The New York Times* was stifled by a strike.

It took death to get Howard Hughes out of hiding in the seventies, so it just seemed as if we were going at everything wrong.

Let's go on to something a little more serious and see if we can't put our fingers on something that will make the eighties a bit better than the last two decades. We have to find our mistakes and do something about them . . . . Here we go one more time, just to see if you can spot something.

In the sixties they marched. In the seventies we jogged. In the sixties we decried injustice. In the seventies we tried to "get in touch with our feelings." After the turmoil of the sixties Americans retreated to purely personal preoccupations . . . to live for the moment was the prevailing passion — to live for yourself, not for your predecessors or anybody else. The seventies were a decade of frustration and alienation. Inflation surged, and identified environmental hazards piled up so quickly that we wrung our hands and moaned that everything seemed to cause cancer.

We worried about cholesterol, our sex lives and our images in the seventies. Kids looked for peak experiences, and got high on mountain air and marijuana, but couldn't spell it. Meanwhile, evangelists of the "how-to movement" fed folks' appetites for self-help. Conservative, fundamentalist religions captalized on an America where there seemed to be nothing left to believe in.

And some time during the seventies, we really began worrying about the future. For the first time the polls showed us to be alarmed. In the sixties, the enemy was communism, and then the war itself. In the seventies, it was the economy we hated. Our response was borrow, buy, and borrow some more. With a greyer tomorrow, we elected to consume while the sun shone. We all wanted to keep "me" happy.

In the seventies Nixon and all spoiled our confidence in elected leaders. The CIA and FBI, long jumped on by radicals, were revealed to the American public as agencies that violated the rights of citizens, by spying, harassing and conspiring to smear. When Watergate wasn't commanding the headlines, wiretaps were. All through the seventies, scandal after scandal screamed from the front pages. Lockheed, ITT, milk producers and Robert Vesco. Boy's Town, the Soap Box Derby and even West Point were portrayed as being rotten. And so, by the end of the decade we'd lost our faith in just about everything. We were out to protect special interests if we got anything out if it. In California, the Proposition 13 was born while the rest of the nation cheered.

In the seventies hair went kinky, and so did sex; at least folks talked about it like they never had before. The Methodists and some other Protestant churches lost millions of members, while evangelical groups attracted them to be born again their way. The celebrities got in on it too, and suddenly everybody was bumping into each other at the baptismal tank. Watergaters Jeb Magruder and Charlie Colson were there. So were Larry Flynt, Eldridge Cleaver and Bob Dylan. We coined the phrase that "Some folks never think of the Lord until he's getting hell licked out of him!" We may have lost faith in government, but many of us found it in some kind of religion.

In the seventies it wasn't the Joneses we worried about keeping up with — it was last year's buying power. Inflation became public enemy number one. We became coupon-clipping misers, hoarding them in every jar in the house. If we found a deal, we pounced on it; if we didn't, we spent our money anyway. In 1979, Americans went over the trillion mark in consumer debt. We were saving less of our incomes, percentage-wise, than we ever had. We adopted the buy-now attitude, figuring that prices could only go up, and it would be better to buy on credit and pay off with inflation-cheapened dollars. We bought, and we bought, and the TV commercials told us what we wanted to hear, "You only go around once in life — grab all the gusto you can."

In the seventies we heard from about everybody with one big exception. The college students — sitting in, standing up and shouting in the sixties — were quiet.

Me? The truth of the matter is that I don't know. Like everyone else, I've been spoiled by the decade of the seventies, of comfort and doing as I pleased. But I do suspect that all this foolishness may be ending. You may still buy appliances, but will there be electricity to run them? Young couples may think twice before bringing their children into a world of DES in the cattle, mercury in the fish and radiation in the air. Heck, you can't afford them anyway.

The fierce sixties burned us out and drove us to thinking only of "me." We have a case of "me madness" in America. During the eighties will we seek a balance of the seventies and sixties? . . . . The sixties with their activism and the seventies with our selfishness . . . . I think we can, but like everybody else, I'm waiting to find out.

Burma Shave

Reading The Signs Passes The Time

It has been said, and I believe it, that you would have to live on Mars if you never saw Joe Engle's phrase, "See Rock City" .... My wife Geri and I were traveling through the deserts of Utah one summer. It was a hot day and being a tenderfoot I didn't carry along any of the necessities that you might need, one of which was water, another was some extra gasoline.

We had been riding all morning without seeing any inhabitants at all. We were running low on gas, and I was getting a little panicky. Finally we saw something up ahead. When we arrived it was a huge bird house. On it was "See Rock City" right out in the middle of the desert.

However, we made it to the next place which sold gas. It was one of those places where no one hung out except Indians. On the roof in big letters was "SEE ROCK CITY." The name of the oasis was "The Middle of the Desert."

I think I must have learned to read by signs like this. While riding along as a young boy I would read aloud any sign which struck my fancy. There were a heap of signs in those days up and down the old 41 highway. Burma Shave signs always attracted me with their witty little jingles. The signs were placed in a row along-side the road. There were usually five with each carrying a line, and the fifth would have the punch line "Burma Shave." I would read the lines aloud and we would get a big kick out of the jingles.

One winter day mama took grandma, grandpa and an aunt along with us to visit some relatives in Whitfield County. I was reading the signs aloud as usual. She's a pretty — She's a lass — Stop in the city — Get off your gas . . . Burma Shave! Well everything was all right except someone had erased the "g" in gas.

81

I was a little embarrassed because I read it like it was. We stayed the night with some relatives who lived in a big old two-story house with high ceilings. When we went to bed there was a roaring fire where my brother and I slept. But the next morning when we got up that house was so cold we grabbed our britches and ran out in the yard to put them on!. . . Like I said today's days just won't come up to days back then.

Remember these "old-timers"?

— Burma Shaves —

A man who drives — While he is drunk — Should haul his coffin — in his trunk — Burma Shave

Don't lose your head — to save a minute — You need your head — Your brains are in it — Burma Shave

Around the curve — Lickity split — It's a beautiful car — Wasn't it? Burma Shave

Cautious Driver — To his reckless dear — Let's have less bull — And a lot more steer — Burma Shave

Don't stick your elbow — Out too far — It might — Ride home — In another car — Burma Shave

Drove too long — Driver snoozing — What happened next — Is not amusing — Burma Shave

Heed instructions — Protect our little — Tax deductions — Burma Shave

Passing cars — Where you can't see — May get you — a glimpse of eternity — Burma Shave

And Grandpa's beard was stiff and coarse — That's what caused — His fifth divorce — Burma Shave

Shaving brush — Is out of date — Use the razor's — Perfect mate — Burma Shave

Whiskers long — Made Samson strong — But Samson's wife — She done him wrong — Burma Shave

His face was smooth — And cool as ice — And, oh, Louise — He smelled so nice — Burma Shave

Shaving Brushes — Will soon be trimmin' — Those screwy hats — We see on women — Burma Shave

Mom & Pop — Are feeling gay — Baby said — As plain as day — Burma Shave

Special seats — Reserved in Hades — For whiskered guys — Who scratch the ladies — Burma Shave

If you dislike — Big traffic fines — Slow down — Til you — Can read these signs — Burma Shave

A peach — Looks good — With lots of fuzz — But man's no peach — And never wuz — Burma Shave

Mirror on — The bathroom wall — What's the — Smoothest Shave — Of all — Burma Shave

Drive like — A railroad engineer — Take it easy — When the road's — Not clear — Burma Shave

Around this curve — You'd better slow — Or you'll be where — The daisies grow — Burma Shave

Driving fast — Because you're late — Doesn't mean — You'll make that date — Burma Shave

If what you want — Is lots of love — Make sure you have — Plenty of — Burma Shave

He played the sax — Had no B. O. — His whiskers scratched — So she let him go — Burma Shave

The bearded lady — Tried a jar — She is now — A movie star — Burma Shave

Listen birds — These signs cost money — So roost a while — But don't get funny — Burma Shave

Riot at drugstore — Calling all cars — 100 customers — Only 99 jars — Burma Shave

And finally —

AS I AM NOW, SO YOU SHALL BE
PREPARE THYSELF TO FOLLOW ME

Underneath which someone wrote:

TO FOLLOW YOU, I'LL NOT CONSENT
UNLESS YOU SAY WHICH WAY YOU WENT

Brush Arbors And
Evergreen Sunday Schools

Mourner's Bench And The Amen Corner

When we talk about the people of the north Georgia mountains of now and how we were, you will note that there just isn't any comparison. The mountain people of the thirties that I remember were deeply religious, or at least everything in life was built around religion. Most of the preachers preached from Paul's letters to Ephesus and the Galatians.

A preacher was supposed to make his living by farming or by some other means, but never take money for preaching. He could be fed or given shelter for the night, and occasionally a hat might be passed to pay some of his expenses. To this day, however, there are many country people who do not like educated preachers who have made the ministry a paid profession.

Just like in the Apostle Paul's letters, the mountain preachers preached against adultery, fornication, uncleanness, lasciviousness, idolatry, witchcraft, hatred, wrath, seditions, heresies, envyings, murders, drunkenness and the like. Others like provoking one another, and if a man thinks himself to be something, when he is nothing, he is deceived. "He thinks he's something, don't he?" became the same as a curse word, or meant about the same thing.

A person was told to "love his neighbors as himself," to "honor his father and mother." This brought about the parents and grandparents living in the homes of their children as a common thing. These things had to be abided by, or the person violating them had a burning hell waiting.

Folks in the mountains back then took extra precaution to obey the Ten Commandments so that they did not generally cheat, lie, or steal. Stealing was hated so bad that is wasn't necessary to lock one's doors. A man's word in any personal dealings was as good as his bond. If anything went wrong with something that he traded, then he made it right. "Thou shalt not bear false witness" was taken seriously. Youth minded his manners and juvenile delinquency was unknown. The Bible was quoted for all behavior, good and bad. Quite often the man quoting would "add to" or take out of context.

87

To this day in the mountains there are no upper, middle and lower classes. There are primarily two classes—sinners and Christians. A good Christian is looked up to far more than any rich man. A man is a sinner until he has been saved or born again.

Now there was quarrelling in the churches. Quite often churches would split. Talking Rock Baptist Church split, with one side holding their meetings in the mornings, while the other side had theirs in the afternoons. They had separate piles of coal for the heater, yet some of the men would fox hunt together but would not sit in church together. This went on for over forty years before one side built another church about six or seven years ago.

Occasionally, a young, fast-talking, well-dressed man who said he was a preacher would come through. He would be a fast talker, causing some of the folk to say, "He shore can preach." He would be popular with the girls, to the local young men's disappointment. Some of the members would be taken for a few bucks, but they never would admit it.

People walked to the "meetings" carrying lanterns. The meetings were a place to release emotional feelings, shouting, praying, crying. A preacher was considered good when he could get the congregation into this state. "Get happy" was the expression, and get happy folks did. The meetings sometimes lasted until two or three in the mornings. They were happy and they enjoyed it. There wasn't much to be happy about in those days.

The Mourner's Bench and Amen Corner were in every church. The Mourner's Bench is where we cried and repented until we were saved. The Amen Corner egged us on and prodded the preacher on, too, or preachers, sometimes five or six, would have a go at it.

In no way am I criticizing. I am only telling some more history that has disappeared from the hills. However, sometimes I find one of these churches and visit and enjoy. One such church is among the rich folks home on top of Tate Mountain, ten miles from my home. It is called Burnt Mountain Baptist Church.

Whenever you have the opportunity, visit a church like we have been talking about. You'll love it and your battery will stay charged for a month.

Funerals Aren't What They Used To Be

Occasionally I help out over at Williard Summey's Furniture Store, mainly because I get to see people whom I haven't seen for a long time. The store is located on Main Street, and if anybody comes to town, there just isn't any way of missing him. Jasper is so small that when we dial a wrong number, we can still chat for an hour or so.

I usually place an old Brumby rocker out in front of the store on warm days, and this is where you can find me if there aren't any customers.

I wasn't surprised when these two women came up to me the other day and told me that they had seen me sitting there as they went to a funeral. They decided to come back by the store and pay me a visit. I was surprised at the way they were dressed, though, because the last time I saw thses ladies was back in the thirties. At that time these two sisters dressed in typical mountain style with high top shoes, bonnets, and always seemed to have a clean apron hanging down the front of their long dresses.

They were now dressed as if they were the "Queen for the Day," and they even talked different from the old-time mountain language. So goes an argument in favor of television if you want to contribute the changes to the tube.

We talked about the person's funeral and I was a little shocked when Miss Laura remarked that she didn't enjoy funerals anymore. Anything about funerals gets to me, but I didn't know anyone enjoyed them until now. In the old days the death ritual was much like that of the Cherokee: it was a time of noisy mourning.

I really don't know when this change took place nor do I exactly remember when the churches did away with the mourner's bench and "Amen Corner" either.

Miss Lucy talked about how neighbors used to "set up" with the body of the deceased for two or three nights before the actual burial took place. The family would talk about how they promised someone something on their deathbed. Really, there was a time here in the mountains that if someone promised somebody something as they lay dying, the request would be respected. You could bet your farm on it, even if the request of the deceased took a person a lifetime to fulfill.

It was Miss Laura's turn to tell how folks would bring food to the house where the person "lay corpse." "Some," she said, "ate better during a mourning than they did in their whole lives." I noticed how she said "ate;" it used to be "et," but I also knew that we were talking about a part in our history just as we talk about the Cherokee.

At the funeral back then, during the singing and the preaching, the family would cry out, sob and moan. But the most emotional scene took place when the casket was opened for that last look. All the family would cry, scream and pray, and sometimes I have seen a person attempt to lie on the casket. Some would kiss the dead person, another might pull at his or her own hair. A lot of them would fall to the floor in convulsions, while other members of the family might faint and have to be carried out. The family would grieve for days before deciding that it was God's will. However, a baby was grieved after for life by the family, just like with the Indians.

They stood up to leave, Miss Laura and Miss Lucy, and I told the biggest lie that I ever told. I said that I "enjoyed" seeing and talking to them. That night I had nightmares all over the place. The old organ that Geri keeps in our living room kept playing over and over by itself, "Amazing Grace," and "In the Sweet Bye and Bye."

A Former Representative's Dream

His name is Ray, or you can call him anything you want as long as you buy him a beer. But Ray one day lay down on a night club floor, having drunk so much he could drink no more. So he fell asleep with a troubled brain, and he dreamed that he rode on a hell-bound train.

The engine with murderous blood was damp and brilliantly lit with a brimstone lamp. An imp, for fuel, was shoveling bones, while the furnace roared with a thousand groans. The boiler was filled with Lager beer, and the devil himself was the engineer. The passengers were a most motley crew. . . .There were church members, atheists, Gentiles and Jews.

There were rich men in four hundred dollar suits, also beggars in rags, beautiful young ladies, and some old withered hags. There were yellow men and black men, red, brown and white, all chained together—Oh, God, what a sight!

While the train rushed on at an awful pace, the sulphurous fumes scorched everybody's face. Bigger and wider the country grew, as faster and faster the engine flew. Louder and louder the thunder crashed, and brighter and brighter the lightning flashed. Hotter and hotter the still air became, till the clothes were burned from each quivering frame.

When out of the distance there rose a yell, "Ha, ha," said the devil. "We're nearing hell!" Then, oh, how the passengers all shrieked with pain and begged the devil to stop the train. But he moved about and danced with glee, and laughed and joked at their misery. "My faithful friends, you have done your work, and ol' satan never can a payday shirk. You've bullied the weak, you've robbed the poor. Your starving brother you've turned from the door. You've laid up gold where the canker rust, and you've given free vent to your beastly lust.

"You've justice scorned, and corruption sown, and trampled the laws of nature down. You have drunk, rioted, cheated, plundered, and lied, and mocked at God in your hell-bound pride. You have paid full fare, so I must carry you through, for it's only right that you should have your due. As the laborer expects his hire I have to land you in the lake of fire.

"Then your flesh will burn in the flames that roar, and my imps will torment you forever more.". . .Then Ray awoke with a pitiful cry, his clothes were wet with sweat and his hair standing up high. . . .

Then he prayed as he had never prayed until that hour, to be saved from his sin and the devil's power. And his prayers and his vows were not in vain, for Ray will never ride that hell-bound train.

What you have just read is a true story, maybe told in an unorthodox way, but Ray, a former state legislator, goes into the "slum rows" and Bourbon Street saving souls. . . .He never tires. . . . He never gives up on anybody all because of a drunken dream. . . . But was it a dream?

You've Come A Long Way Baby, But You've Still Got A Long Way To Go

Their Women Obeyed

It happens all the time: a couple who have lived for the past thirty-five or forty years in some other section of the United States moves back to the mountains, expecting to pick up their childhood where it was left off. They have worked hard, saving for a dream to retire to the place where they knew life in its simplest form.

It seldom works out, though, because they have kept it in the back of their minds that the civilization in the mountains stood still while they made their modest fortunes in an industrialized, educated and economically sound section of the country.

Our language and customs used to be different from any other part of the state. Atlanta, although only sixty miles away, was in a foreign country to most mountaineers. It hasn't been so long ago when people here took eggs or produce to the store to trade for sugar or something that couldn't be grown on their hilly one-horse farms.

Wives walked eight or ten steps behind their husbands, usually "toting" whatever they were taking for barter. In those days, a wife was silent, obeyed her husband and served him. She did not disagree with him, and she and her daughters served the husbands and sons. When the man finished, the women ate. In church, she sat on the other side of the aisle from him with the other women. She was allowed no voice in the meetings.

Girls learned how to change diapers, butcher hogs, comfort the dying, take orders, pitch manure and cook a tasty meal. The only education necessary was how to "back a letter" and how to read the Bible. Math was unnecessary; this was men's doings.

A seventh grade education in a one-room schoolhouse with one teacher was good enough for any mountain boy or girl. Sometimes, one would stay in the seventh grade for several terms, or until a boy was much older than the teacher.

"Know the seventh grade," children were told, "and you will be equal to a college graduate."

Folks talked different, too. They "hoped out" instead of helped. It was "kiver" for cover in most homes, and a "poke" was a bag. A bull was called a "brute," even when a man was talking to his wife. Anything different was "quare," and a dog was told to "beguine" for begone. A spotted cow or horse was "piedy," and a snake "quiled" to strike instead of coiled.

During those days of the simple life, the rural folks were deeply religious in their own way. The husband was the head of the house, never to be disagreed with under his roof. I suppose this was taken from the Apostle Paul's letter to the Ephesians, "Wives, submit yourselves unto your husbands, as unto the Lord. For the husband is the head of the wife."

It mattered not to them that Paul was a bachelor, and I suspect a "hardheaded" one, this was the Word of the Bible and had to be carried out. And any wrong-doing, no matter how minor, was tended to by some older man quoting scripture, sometimes out of context, and sometimes "added to," but the man doing the Bible-quoting was respected as a man whom God had touched.

An outsider was never accepted, even up until the fifties, and to a certain extent today. A man who has lived here for fifteen years and offers himself for public office soon finds that out. One had to be born here, descended from here, or marry someone from here before the door was opened. New folks were looked upon as "braggerts" and undercover Revenue Agents. Sometimes a stranger was looked upon as a German spy.

Most babies were birthed with the help of a mid-wife. A child was taught to honor his father. Even if the father was a drunkard or too sorry to work, the wife protected him. "He's your father and you will not speak disrespectful to him," were her words. The Whites named their children for Gene Talmadge, and the Blacks named theirs for Roosevelt.

The folks who come home again find everything changed. Most folks talk like an English professor. The mountains have been industrialized to the point that you don't know when you leave Pickens County and get to Atlanta. Beautiful houses now cover the mountains, and everything is just as up to date as any other place in America. They will buy a house, hang around for a while, before soon moving back to where they came from.

I feel sorry for them because in my selfish way, I sometimes get a hankering for that simple life when nobody had anything and didn't want "nuthin." But then I think of seeing an old woman sitting on the porch of an old run-down house, the red lines of her hands caused by years of labor, her face lined from years of worry, her eyes sometimes red with tears. But she was a good cook. This was her life's ambition.

I wouldn't want this simple life for my daughters. . . .I doubt if a state senator or representative would either, but it is he who is so noble as to protect a woman from anything—except himself.

ERA: It's Only American

Has it really been nine years? Man, time sure does get by. Nine years since Congress proposed to the states the Equal Rights Amendment, or more accurately, the Women's Rights Amendment, and (as illustrated by the Georgia Senate defeat of ERA last year) it still hangs in limbo.

This was not expected in 1972. Within a few days of congressional approval, Hawaii approved it. In the next two years, nineteen other states added their approval. By 1974, the total was thirty-four. Only four more states were needed to ratify it to become the twenth-seventh amendment since the Constitution was adopted in 1789; and it was thought that would soon be forthcoming. Not so, but one other state has approved, making the total thirty-five, needing only three states' approval to ratify.

What the proposed amendment says is simply that "equality of rights under the law shall not be denied or abridged by the United States or by any state on account of sex." But to some, there are a number of booby traps lurking behind those simple words.

It has been said, for example, that ERA would make it illegal to have separate toilets in public places for men and women, that it would void state laws making it a crime to rape women or seduce girls under sixteen. That husbands would not be held responsible for supporting wives and children. And that women could no longer be exempted from military duty in time of war, even in combat.

These fears are as farfetched, in my opinion, as the one about mixed toilets. If the ERA were adopted, there would be a long period where the courts would have to untangle all the present laws from the constitutional provision. It's been two hundred years, and some of the amendments aren't enforced yet. But "equal rights under the law" doesn't always mean, in either law or common sense, identical rights.

Statutes regulating abortions will not be struck down on the grounds that such laws do not apply to men. Nor will laws designed to determine fatherhood be cancelled because they do not apply to women. No court, in my opinion, will apply the language of the law to achieve an absurdity. No court wants to go down in history as being idiotic.

Some laws beneficial to women will survive so long as there is justification for their continuance. There are differences between men and women that the law cannot eliminate nor ignore. All the ERA does is affirm in constitutional language a philosophical principle — that women are not to be denied the rights and privileges of full citizenship in their community simply because they are women.

Many other principles stated in the Constitution — like the right of speech or a fair trial — are still a long way down the road to fulfillment, and may never be. Out country is built on philosophic principles such as the ERA. "All men are created equal" was something along these lines; and in fact, it took one hundred years to free the slaves. Indians were completely ignored; and, ol' buddies, there it is right there in our Constitution.

If you are worrying about these changes coming tomorrow, don't! It took over one hundred years to make it a reality that the right to vote should not be denied because of race, creed or color. As for women, two hundred years ago, they could not vote, hold office, serve on juries, own property or even act as guardian to their very own children. As late as one hundred years ago, they could not practice law or medicine. It was only fifty-odd years ago when they won the right to vote.

Ours has been a long journey toward a philosophical principle that women are fighting for and should be given, and making "all men" mean "all mankind."

During our bicentennial in 1976, we told the world over and over that all persons in the United States are equal in their rights under our laws. It is a barefaced lie, and everyone in America knows it.

Statistics show that men and women are struck by lightning with the same frequency, that it rains and the sun shines on both. So to even things up, give the women their philosophical principle. The same kind of principle that our whole Constitution is based upon.

 ## Reasons For Being Sure To Vote Today

She was fifty years old when she voted for the first time. The year was 1948, only three years after her son was killed in World War II. She said that she always looked on voting as "men's doings" until that day her son's casket was brought home for burial. It was what the preacher said that made her change her outlook on elections, and what it meant to have the privilege of casting a ballot.

The preacher was attempting to explain why her son died. Thousands of Americans had died on the battlefields just so we could preserve our democracy. "All a democracy is," he said, "is the right to vote and choose our leaders." He went on to tell the folks that America is one of the few countries in the world where the citizens select their officials by elections.

The preacher said other things, too, but she made up her mind that day that she would vote in every election for the rest of her life. She has, too, and now at the age of eighty-two, she told me that she would be at the polls today to vote in the presidential primary for Jimmy Carter, her fellow Georgian.

It was a long journey down a rough road that women won the right to vote. They have had this privilege for only a few years, yet only a small number of women exercise this right. There is talk that something has happened lately to make all women use their right to vote. According to rumblings, there will probably be more women voting in today's presidential primary than have ever voted before.

Blacks as well as a lot of whites went through some mean years just so blacks could vote in Georgia's primaries. You would have thought that after all this, every black in Georgia would have "bust" the door down to vote in any kind of election. This hasn't been the case, as statistics will show. Only a small percentage of blacks has been voting.

According to my source, blacks, too, are sitting up and taking more notice of what they have been missing by not casting a ballot. These folks are making plans to vote in today's primary to show the world that they weren't just fooling around when they were fighting for this right.

If my information is correct, and I have no reason to doubt it, we may see the heaviest turnout in today's election that has ever been witnessed in Georgia.

A psychologist who studied in Germany says that Russia thinks the United States is not as united because of people failing to show up to vote in presidential races. Nobody can lose an election bet in Russia; and according to the good doctor, the average Russian thinks the American people might even favor their type of government. "Heavy turnouts in elections," he says, "will cause the Soviets more worry than all the battleships we can float in the Indian Ocean."

Jane Byrne, mayor of Chicago, recently said that she would not grant the Irish a permit to parade on St. Patrick's Day. The reason this wild woman gave was because the Irish had invited President Carter. "Carter is not Irish," she said. "He is a Georgia Cracker." Byrne used the term as a derogatory slur.

President Carter has supported the women's movements, so one would have to assume that the women will support him, especially since Ted Kennedy reminds many women of one of their own who is not as fortunate as the ones who are alive to vote today.

President Carter has put blacks in the highest positions in government of any former president, and he did it out of sincerity, too. He didn't have his arm around blacks' shoulders while his FBI chief was trying to discredit their leader like some folks did in the past.

Now, if we turn out at the polls in heavy numbers to show the Soviets that we are united, and if we turn out to honor those who died just so we can vote, Georgia is bound to have more people voting today than in any previous election. Besides, there are those of us who want to show the mayor of Chicago what it really means to be a "Georgia Cracker" by giving Jimmy Carter the biggest vote any presidential candidate ever got in Georgia.

Ninth District Congressman Ed Jenkins sized the situation up like this, when he endorsed Jimmy Carter for a second term, "The president hasn't had a 'Bay of Iran.' I'm glad that he has done such a good job, because I don't want it to be another one hundred years before we have another president from Georgia." None of us do, congressman. None of us do.

How About Holidays For The Indians

When I was a little kid, a big kid made me eat some dirt. I didn't like the taste of it and I haven't eaten any since. When I was sixteen some of my white peers beat me up because I was for Joe Louis instead of the German, Schmeling. The beating I got wasn't near as bad as losing the fifty cents on the fight that I made working in a warehouse all the night before, sorting potatoes.

On June 22, 1938, I was still outspoken in favor of Joe over Schmeling, but this time I didn't have fifty cents to lay on him. After the fight which a gang of us had listened to on the radio up at Lawson's Garage, once again four white boys ganged me on the way home and I received a few bumps and bruises.

It has always been my belief that blacks should have their respective place in this world, just like I do not believe a woman should be deprived of full citizenship in her community just because she is a woman. However, no matter how much a person is for equality, if he is against something blacks are for, no matter how trifle, he is called a racist.

I was against the NAACP when they wanted to take *Amos and Andy* off television. I was raised listening to this program on radio and had begun to feel it was a part of me. And busing, I was against that too. I believe even today that when historians get it all written down that busing will be looked back on as the stupidest thing civilized people ever did, no matter what side you are on.

I would be the first to say that Martin Luther King Jr. was probably the most courageous man of the century. Being one who respects courage I like to see schools and places named for him. I like to see efforts made in his behalf for the underprivileged, and I applaud when someone erects a monument to him.

But, doggone it, about this making it a holiday on the day King was born is a little far fetched to me. In the first place any holiday just means that government employees get the day off while everybody else has to work. In the second place, no matter how great a man is, he should take his proper place in line for anything.

102

Most of us up here in the mountains have Indian blood. It is my opinion that the race of the red men suffered more humiliation than any other race. Yet, the Indians had their heroes too — Sequoia, the man of the alphabet, and John Ross, just to mention a couple of Cherokees. I am sure there also are supporters in favor of making the birthdays of Geronimo, Sitting Bull, Crazy Horse and many others a holiday.

I am not opposed to the Martin Luther King holiday so much that I'm going to make speeches about it, but when they talk about honoring people there are some who should not be forgotten. Once again it just depends on what side you're on. I'm not going to mention people like the Kennedys, Ralph McGill, Roosevelts and others whose supporters would like to see a holiday to honor them on their birthday. But, when everybody else gets a holiday in their honor, please try to consider some of my ancestors.

Even then it would probably be like the first treaty signed by the white man and the Indian, which read: "The Indian can stay on this land as long as the river runs and the sun sets, or thirty days, whichever comes first."

Stranger In The Night

Superstition Is Foolish, But Free

It's still a little hard for me to place in my mind that the Atlanta Police Department sent for a psychic to help solve the murders of several black children.

Atlanta's police department is supposed to be one of the biggest in the country. Many of the high brass is imported from California and other states. These men are well educated and it just doesn't seem possible that they would believe in fortune telling enough to think that a woman had some kind of power that the rest of us don't have. I thought such thinking went out with high top shoes.

Of course, events occur at times to make you believe such nonsense until you have time to think it over. And there is the old one-liner of mine that superstition is foolish, childish, primitive and irrational, but it don't cost nothing to knock on wood.

Blanche Jones wrote a column for this paper back during the forties. I have enjoyed reading her pieces very much, because she is a very talented writer. I never met Miss Jones, but I feel as though I know her after reading the old files of *The North Georgia Tribune* so much lately. She is so good that I'm surprised that there isn't a book around somewhere with her name on it, if "Jones" is still her name.

Blanche picked up a piece from *The Atlanta Journal* and reprinted it in her column from November 3, 1941. Now the story is hard to believe no matter who wrote it, but in 1941 we believed that anything that was in print to be the gospel. It just never occurred to us that a story would be published in an Atlanta paper unless it were true. Anyway, here is Blanche's reprint.

107

It happened in Atlanta on Halloween night, a couple were returning home via Stewart Avenue from a party. It was rather late or early in the morning as the case may be, and if you remember Halloween night, it was a rainy, weird night, just suited to the occasion.

As they were riding down Stewart Avenue, they spied a girl sitting on the curb, clad in a silver, shimmery evening dress, a little worse for the rain, and crying her heart out. They stopped and the boy asked if he could be of any help. The girl replied that he could carry her home if he would and gave him an address on Peachtree Road.

The boy got out, helped the girl into the two-door car, and started on his way. He and his date tried to engage the girl in a conversation, but she didn't seem very talkative, so they gave it up.

When they arrived at the address she had given him, the boy got out of the car to help the girl out, but there was no girl back there. She had been sitting in the back seat and there was no other way possible for her to get out of the car except by climbing over either the boy or girl in the front seat. The windows were all shut to keep out the rain but it hadn't kept the girl in the car. She just wasn't there.

The boy thought that needed some explaining so he went up to the door and rang the bell to report such an oddity. Finally, a little grey-haired lady came to the door. The boy explained to her the best as he could, the circumstances and the lady asked for a description of the girl. After the boy supplied it she said,

"That was my daughter. You are the fourth couple who have been here tonight to bring her home. She was killed four years ago tonight in an automobile wreck out on Stewart Avenue."

Just Waiting For Her Son

It was just before Christmas when the letter came from Mrs. Madeline Caine. She was a resident of a nurse care home in Atlanta and wanted to tell me about some things. The letter was so well composed and the handwriting was so beautiful I thought perhaps someone had written it for her. I don't know why I thought this, since I had never heard of her, but there is something about one of those homes that I associate anybody as old and disabled who lives there.

I soon learned different because within the next few days I happened to be in that vicinity and dropped in for a visit with her. She was an attractive lady, probably in her late seventies, well-dressed, her hair well groomed and she had on make-up giving the impression that she wasn't ready to quit living, not yet anyway. We sat down in the neat visiting room, furnished with nice furniture and a color television set. There were other visitors, but the room was so large that you hardly noticed.

Mrs. Caine was mentally alert, too much, I thought, for her to be here in this place. I liked to hear her talk. Her grammar was excellent and she had a manner of speaking which made you want to listen. I was impressed by how much she knew about current events and she told me that she read both *The Atlanta Journal* and *The Constitution* daily. She went to her room and brought a handful of clippings from the op-ed page of the *Constitution* depicting a picture of a white-haired writer, which really did impress me.

She was born in Fannin County, Georgia in 1912. Her father, a scientist, was employed by the copper company across the Tennessee line. She graduated from high school there before her family moved to New York where her father went with the Dupont Company. She told me about the girls in college who disbelieved her when she told them that she had never seen a black or cotton growing. "Anybody from Georgia," they laughed, "knows all about blacks and fields of cotton." I knew this to be the truth as my background is in the same area.

She graduated from college and married Julius Abbott Caine, a scientist like her father. The Caines moved to Atlanta where Mrs. Caine taught school until Julius Abbott Caine III came along on February 2, 1947. She had a hard time in labor and I listened patiently until Abbott started to school. I understood all of this, I have a seven-year-old grandson myself. Abbott never fooled around with any drugs or anything like that and finished the University in 1968 before beginning his military duty. A picture of a young, handsome lieutenant was the next thing she showed me.

There was something about this lady that intrigued me as I sat there listening to some of the most elegant talk that I have ever heard. Her husband died of a heart attack on May 8, 1969, and she had gone back to teaching to help pass the time and supplement her income. She was visiting friends in New York when she became ill and was hospitalized there for two months. Her son came home from the Army, she said, to help her. She recovered from this illness and returned to her home in Atlanta. She began losing weight and the doctors couldn't find her trouble. She had to resign her teaching job in 1974.

Mrs. Caine became a hospital volunteer and did many other things for the next four years. Her son married, she said, but he called her every night just before she went to bed. "He's so good to me," she said. She became seriously ill a couple of years ago and couldn't look after herself. Her son came home and he and her pastor sold her house and made arrangements for her to live here in the nurse care home.

Abbott and his wife had a son by this time and Mrs. Caine had never seen her grandson. Abbott couldn't get home for Christmas, but he is bringing his family to see her on January 12. The lady was so thrilled that I laughed a lot with her. I too was glad that she was going to know what a grandson is really like. Plans had been made for her to leave the nurse care home, and they were all going to Florida for a month. I don't think that I have ever been as happy for anyone as I bade her farewell. "I'll be back," I said.

I went by there the other day and asked to see Mrs. Caine. I nearly went into shock when the nurse told me that Mrs. Caine passed away on January 12.

"My Lord," I said, "Did her son get here?"

"She had no son," came the reply. "He was killed in the Vietnam War on May 8, 1969."

Ordinary And Unordinary

Let's relate some ordinaries to other ordinaries today and see what we come up with. Back in 1974 we found out that some eighteen minutes were missing from certain tapes made by Richard Nixon. Well, back in 1865, the year Abraham Lincoln was shot, his assassin, John Wilkes Booth, also was killed. On him was found a diary which was turned over to Secretary of War William Stanton. When Stanton released it, some eighteen pages were missing. That makes for two "eighteen" omissions that may have changed the history of our United States.

Another: Since William Henry Harrison was elected President in 1840 and died only months after his inauguration, every President elected on the first year of a new decade has died in office. This is such a year.

After Harrison, the Presidents who took office at the beginning of decades and died in office were Lincoln (1860), Garfield (1880), McKinley (1900), Harding (1920), Roosevelt (1940) and Kennedy (1960).

This may sound morbid and even in bad taste, but a statistic is a statistic. A trend — a very, very strange trend — has been going on, unbroken, for one hundred and forty years; and now there is a chance, a slim one, but a chance, that the country could elect a seventy year old man as President. Of course, if he were elected to a second term, then he'd be pushing eighty in his second term. I don't suppose this means anything unless you're superstitious. But considering that the average life expectancy of the American male is 69.3, we'd better hope that (just in case he is elected) Reagan chooses a real humdinger of a running mate.

Reagan likes jelly beans, according to the media. Maybe he is in that second you-know-what; but anyway, he has been known to make the statement that it is ignorant to be superstitious. Well, maybe so, but it don't cost nothing to knock on wood.

But in all fairness, I must repeat, "Old age is a funny thing to me. I know some men old at forty . . . and some young at seventy three."

111

Singing In The Rain

Old Glory In The Rain

I suppose one of the saddest stories that I have heard lately came out of Mississippi.

It seems that James R. Cloudland was arrested and put in jail for stealing an American flag. Other charges were placed against Cloudland for destruction of government property. Mr. Cloudland cut the rope on the flagpole so "Old Glory" would fall down into his arms, and then he jumped in his car and vamoosed. A post office employee watched the whole maneuver with astonishment and got the tag number of the thief's car. When the culprit was apprehended some time later in a beer joint, the stolen flag was still in his car.

James Cloudland, a veteran of World War II, explained the situation thus: it was raining and the flag of the United States was soaking wet up on that pole. He had been taught to treat the flag with more respect than that, so he cut the rope and took the flag to teach the post office a lesson.

What Cloudland didn't know was that the rules for flying the flag had been changed drastically since 1942. This is the fault of the press and most of the blame can be put on the Veterans Administration for not educating the public on these changes.

Legislation enacted during the U.S. Bicentennial year of 1976 revised, for the first time in 34 years, the rules governing the use and display of the American flag. Amendments to the flag code were introduced to clear up some misunderstandings regarding proper flag etiquette and attention which had developed since 1942 when the law was written.

The amended code permits around the clock display of the flag when properly lighted at night, and the flying of the colors in inclement weather when an all-weather flag is used. This amendment came about as a result of developments in weather resistant material for flags.

A section of the old code requiring a flag to be firmly affixed to the radiator cap when displayed on an automobile was amended so that the flag must now be attached to the right front fender. This change is obvious, since there are no radiator caps on the outside of the hoods of automobiles anymore.

The code still requires men to remove their head dress with their right hand and hold it at the left shoulder, the hand being over the heart when saluting the flag. But, the line requiring women to salute by placing the right hand over the heart was deleted. And the revised code gives new life to Old Glory. The code now states: "The flag represents a loving country and is itself considered a living thing."

So what Mr. Cloudland didn't know was that he could have been charged with kidnapping the flag, which in effect can carry the death penalty.

When the judge learned the circumstances of the flag stealing case, he dismissed the charges. He then asked for donations to replace the rope on the flagpole, the flag still being intact and not damaged. Pardon me. . .I mean "hurt," since the flag is a living thing.

Everybody in town turned out to see the winner of the bronze star and two purple hearts repair the flag so that it could be raised again. The crowd was saluting with hats over their hearts as the flag went up, but they also roared. You see, it was raining like hell.

Remembering Ducktown

In the year 1930 bridge-playing was a madness. The popular songs of the day were "I Got Rhythm," "Three Little Words," "Time on My Hands," "Walking My Baby Back Home," and "On the Sunny Side of the Street." Herbert Hoover was President, and the Great Depression was now taking a big bite in America.

I was ten years old and living in Ducktown, Tennessee, a mining town which attracted the attention of many papers as a town that had not been tamed and never would be. They were right on both counts.

"Miners Homecoming Day" in Copperhill and Ducktown is the day that most everybody who has moved away returns for the celebration. Big names in the country and western music business will be there, and I have been asked to autograph *Mountain Echoes* at the museum on Main Street in Ducktown.

Of course I'm going. It brings back good memories. There were five of us boys. I was the youngest. My daddy worked for the Tennessee Copper Company for forty years, and later two brothers went to work for the company. Earl, the next to the oldest, worked until he retired and became ill just a few days later. He was in Copper Basin Hospital.

I drove up there every day to be with him. As I sat there in that lonely hospital room my mind went back to 1930 when a tent show came to town. Earl took me to the show with a fifty-cent piece.

Earl, Bob Rimer and Moony Miller were football players on the Ducktown squad, and take my word for it, you can't get any tougher than that. They left me to myself. I bought a hot dog and paid the fat lady with my money, but she didn't give me back my forty cents change. I asked her about this, and she insisted that she had. I protested politely, so she reached over and got my weiner and threw it in the sawdust.

Earl, Bob and Mooney came up about that time and told the fat woman to give me my money back. She didn't. Instead, she called out "Hey Rube!" This brought three men who looked like gorillas.

Earl hit one under the chin, raising him off the ground two feet. Bob cracked the other two men's heads together while Mooney grabbed a sledge hammer and began to knock down the stakes that held the tent. It fell, wrapping around the woman who had caused the trouble.

Deputy "Stiff Arm" Thomas came up, and the owner of the show demanded that the boys be arrested. As soon as "Stiff Arm" heard my story he took out his pistol and fired twice into the air. He gave the show people ten minutes to get out of town. "And I don't mean eleven either," he growled.

That's as fast as I've ever seen trucks loaded. When Thomas heard the fat woman still had my fifty cents, he took off after the trucks with Earl, Bob and Mooney hanging on his fender. They brought my money back.

It was along about daylight when I watched my brother fight for his last breath . . . . While visiting the hospital I had learned that both Bob and Mooney had passed on some years before . . . . I was scared until I heard Bob whisper, "Pass the word, Mooney, ole Earl is here!"

Ducktown Homecoming

Due to so many phone calls it is essential that I give a report on The Miners Homecoming at Ducktown, Tennessee, the week of July 1. To say the least the celebration was a tremendous success with hundreds of people parading through the town and museum.

People came from Deleware, Arizona, California and from all over the state of Tennessee. Your's Truly was busy most of the day autographing three hundred copies of my new book *Mountain Echoes*. The book has some stories about some of the wildness of Ducktown during the thirties. This accounts for what happens next.

Some of the folks recalled some of the gunfights which took place on Main Street, and Mrs. Claudia Beckler called off fifteen men who were there. I was pretty busy when someone yelled that a gunfight was about to take place outside in the street. The atmosphere was just right because of the discussion that was taking place about some of the things that had happened.

I went to the window of the museum and saw two rough looking characters with beards eye-balling one another at a distance of fifteen feet; others wore guns, and it was apparent that something was about to take place. Guns were drawn and one of the men went down as shots rang out. Gary Cooper in *High Noon* couldn't have done it better. Everything was quiet, and suddenly the man who was down got up. My heart was in my mouth because I expected more shooting, but instead people looked at me and started laughing. The townsfolk had set the whole thing up just for my benefit.

This may seem strange that I was excited, but these things still happen occasionally in the mining town. Some say that it's a little tamer than it used to be, which I questioned. I had heard a guy say that they were stopping people down at the city limits and searching them for a gun. If they didn't have one, they gave them one.

The preacher at Jasper seemed to doubt some of the stories. I assured him that about anything you wanted to tell happened in Ducktown some time or other. I told him about the salesman who stopped his car in front of a cafe one day. He asked the waitress what folks did in this hick town for excitement. The words were no sooner said when gunfire was heard outside in the street. Two deputies caught a former deputy in a crossfire, and it took the undertaker a while to count the holes in the ex-deputy. The salesman jumped in his car and took off hurridly toward Chattanooga.

A picnic was given for my family by the townfolks up on the hill near the mines where my daddy worked for so long. It was about sundown as we got in our station wagon for the trip home. The setting sun was shining at an angle on the red hills blending in jewel-like colors of turquoise, emerald and topaz, taking on the look of the deserts of Arizona.

Our six-year-old grandson is still talking about the gunfight and the place that looks like it's a movie set for an old western . . . like I said, you can tell anything you want to about Ducktown, Tennessee, because some time or other it really happened . . . . It's best that you and the preacher go see for yourself.

Depression Years Created Friends

It was during the Great Depression. The year was 1935. I was sixteen years old. There were very few jobs for men, and soup lines were common in the cities. Old Highway 41 was bumper to bumper with traffic most of the time, mostly with Dixie-Ohio Express trucks. The highway went right through the heart of Dalton. Once in a while someone would be arrested so the policemen could be paid. Them Yankees were easier to pick than cotton.

These were the lean years. H.L. Godfrey was singing with a gospel group on the Chattanooga radio station. Mule Shirley was playing first base for the Lookouts. Babe Ruth had retired the year before. Nobody locked their doors when they went off, but nobody had anything worth stealing.

I was living at Talking Rock and figured out a way to make a little money. I removed the back seat from our car and would journey to Dalton for a load of spreads. They weren't spreads yet. They had been laid out to be tufted by hand. I would load up my car and bring them to Pickens County, distributing them to the women in the county along with the different colors of thread that the company provided.

Later I would go pick up the completed hand tufted spreads, paying the women fifteen cents each. Then I would take them back to Dalton where I would receive a quarter and sometimes thirty cents for them. I bought a new Plymouth, paying for it with the money I earned on the counter pins. That's what us ol' country folks called them. (Does anyone know why?) But the Deluxe Plymouth just cost six hundred and ninety dollars.

During this period two things happened that stick with me. A truck driver stopped at a truck stop between Calhoun and Dalton. He ordered pie and coffee. Three Hell's Angels were in the cafe. They went over to the trucker's booth. One began to eat his pie while another drank his coffee. The third motorcycler played with a heavy chain.

The truck driver didn't say anything, but paid the waitress and left. One of the men said to the waitress. "He ain't much of a man, is he?"

"He ain't much of a driver, either," replied the waitress. "He just ran over three motorcycles!"

No jobs. People were hungry. Sometimes a man would hear that they were hiring away off somewhere. He would hitchhike or hobo to get there only to be disappointed when he found that it was just a rumor of hope. He would return home worse off than when he left.

One man in Dalton who had been laid off at the mill moved his family to an old run-down farm near Center Point. They went to work cleaning off the branch banks, sweeping off the yard with straw brooms. Even white washed the old unpainted house.

The preacher came calling on his new neighbors. After oohing and aahing he remarked, "The Lord sure has done wonders for this old place!"

"Yes," replied the farmer, "but he didn't do nothing with it before I moved down here!"

Sure those were lean years, but people visited and they shared. Perhaps there was a closeness then that we will never experience again. Today we have about anything we want, but today's days just won't come up to days back then.

Each Person Charts His Own Course

Larry and his mother moved from Canton to Atlanta in 1925. He was eight at the time, but said he could remember people talking about how dry it was. That was the last time Larry saw Cherokee County. The mother and son moved into an old unpainted house on what was then Fair Street, now known as Memorial Drive.

Fair Street was in the shadow of Georgia's Capitol building, yet it was lined with dilapidated houses, which by today's standards would be called a ghetto. The neighborhood was known as the home of "one dollar women," and a steady stream of men and boys paraded up and down the sidewalks.

They would laugh and joke about anything with the girls sitting on the porches of their houses. Occasionally, a man would hold up one finger, and the woman on the porch would nod her head in the affirmative, and the two would enter the house together.

Larry was born with one foot shorter than the other. When he walked down the sidewalk, it seemed as if he had one foot in the gutter as he hobbled along, but that's just the way he walked. He said that he never knew his father or what had happened to him. During the Depression, Larry was seen picking up produce around the Capitol that the farmers had discarded. This area was the only "farmer's market" of the day, and the men of the soil would park their old vehicles around the Capitol and sell their crops.

Sometimes, a farmer would become discouraged when he didn't have many customers, and would drive off, leaving his vegetables. Larry would hop on to a deal like this, and picking up those discarded vegetables is how he and his mother survived. That is, until she was taken to the tuberculosis hospital in Rome, where she soon died.

123

He attended grammar school down on Pryor Street, but dropped out for good at age eleven. Larry would make book for two dollar bets and sold some "bug tickets," finally making enough money to move into a boarding house near Twelfth Street. These were hard times in Dixie, so Larry sold magazine subscriptions door-to-door, along with having other odd jobs.

Time marched right on, and so did the Depression. A policeman who was a friend of Larry's urged him to enroll in Smith Hughs Vocational School, which he did at the age of twenty.

Larry's hangout became the Carnegie Library instead of York's Pool Room. He read everything he could lay his hands on, and won the gold medal at school for spelling. He met and married a schoolmate, who also walked with a limp. They lived together in one room on what Larry made at his odd jobs. He finished school with honors and could type sixty words a minute.

Larry went to work for Standard Oil as a clerk typist. Over the years, the rest is history. He and his wife, Marion, moved to Dallas, where he soon formed his own independent oil company and became extremely wealthy.

Marion and Larry were afraid to have children at first, but ended up with three strong, healthy boys. They were good parents, giving parental love to the boys as they grew up. They all attended church and Sunday School each week.

This might sound rather strange, because by all the odds against Larry, he should have grown up to lead a life of crime and years in prison, or even the electric chair. So you see, a child doesn't have to go bad just because he doesn't have a color TV.

On the other hand, the sad part is that Larry tried to buy his boys everything that he missed while growing up. The children were flooded with toys while they were tots, and there were sports cars aplenty when they reached high school. Money was always jingling in the boys' pockets, and Larry even opened large bank accounts for each of them.

Yet, all three boys today are serving long terms in prison — one for murder, one for bank robbery and the youngest for a whole bunch of crimes. It just goes to show you — ships don't always run the course they have been charted to run.

People Not Different, Just Reporting

It has been over fifty years since I've heard from Secretary Hawkins. "Sec" was the chubby little boy in a serial, in some publication which has escaped my memory. The story was built around some boys who had a club in a houseboat on the river at the edge of town.

The story led to Secretary Hawkins Clubs being formed all across the country. Each week, the story would leave our hero in a desperate situation, chasing "Link" or someone who had broken into the club. After the "To be concluded," we would wait anxiously until the next week to see what happened.

During this same age, the movie shown at the "Y" would have a two-reel serial preceding the Hoot Gibson cowboy movie. Mrs. Fred Kimsey, the wife of the local doctor, would play the piano during the silent film, and occasionally stop to read the words on the screen aloud to us. Each week, the serial would leave our hero in a predicament, and this would be the topic of conversation until the next Saturday night, predicting what was going to happen.

During the thirties, mothers would stay glued to the radio, listening to serials such as *Ma Perkins, Pepper Young's Family*, or *Stella Dallas*. As soon as the play ended with "Tune in next week to see what happens," the women would crank their telephones and discuss the characters in the serials as if they knew them. Even at the quilting parties, Stella, Pepper or Ma would be discussed along with the new schoolteacher or new preacher.

In Nathanial Reinhardt's *Diary*, he tells about his father subscribing to *The New York World* in 1878. The Reinhardts lived in a remote section of Cherokee County that is now known as Waleska, Georgia. The paper came weekly by Star Route from Cartersville to Sharp's Store at Waleska, where Nath went three miles to pick it up. "Along about fodder pulling time," wrote

Nath (the son of Lewis Reinhardt, founder of the college by the same name), "a serial story commenced, by the title of *A Divided House* or *The Red Manse Mystery*. The scene was the mighty West; there were cowboys, Indians and bucking broncos aplenty, and the thing was written in a way to stimulate and increase interest to the end.

"Before long, the whole settlement knew about this story; and on Sunday afternoons, the adults and larger children gathered at our house to hear me read the installments. None of us had ever heard of fictional literature, and to all of us, the story was intensely real. There would have been no way to convince us that the author, or anyone else, could have invented or have been allowed to publish, such an elaborate lie.

"Finally, just before the expiration date of our subscription, an installment, instead of winding up with the customary 'To be continued in our next' changed to 'To be concluded in our next.' Also, the very status of the story required that something pop. The hero was beleaguered by danger. It was for him a funeral or a wedding, with the odds in favor of the funeral.

"The paper came to the store on Friday afternoons, and so at noon on Friday, my father stopped the plow and told me to go for the mail. When I reached the store, I saw quite an unusual crowd. I hitched and went up on the store porch and saw the crowd was made up of my audience for the run of the story. The instant I saw their faces, I knew that they had beat me to it, and had the paper read by the clerk, who was the only one who could read also, and that the story had ended in tragedy. Finally, Tom Coster approached me and said, 'Nath, he's dead.' Then, he walked away to conceal his grief and tears."

But I have read that over three hundred years ago, when Richardson's novel, *Pamela*, was being read serially in a backwoods community in England, and when, at his conclusion, he brought his heroine, a poor working girl, triumphantly through temptation into honorable and desirable marriage, the sympathetic reader and listeners rushed into town and rang the town bell. Another interested gent who had fallen in love with Pamela as the story was read, hanged himself after learning of her marriage.

Just goes to show you that people are no different from the way they've always been. Newspaper reporting is just better.

Pete And Repeat

Atlanta was like any other southern city in 1938. The town seemed lazy during the day, but from four o'clock until dark it was the noisiest place you ever saw. It was the same in the early mornings with a thousand car horns blowing at the same time, and the clang-clank of the streetcars could be heard over the car sounds. On Sundays, there was very little stirring around the city, and it was the lonesomest place a person could be.

There were very few jobs, even less money as the Depression deepened. I was about nineteen at the time and left the mountains for the city to seek my fortune, as the saying goes. Acquiring a room at the YMCA for $1.50 a week, I picked up any kind of job that came along, knowing that some day me and Horatio Alger would make it to the top.

Across the street from the "Y" stood the Baptist Tabernacle where I spent Sunday mornings listening to Morgan Blake, sports editor of the *Atlanta Journal* teach a Sunday School class. Afterwards, I would run as fast as one could to get to Pierce Harris' Methodist Church before services began.

Dr. Harris and Morgan befriended me on several occasions, and it was through them that I landed a temporary job for the Christmas holidays at a local department store as a store detective. The job was to apprehend shoplifters and either call a policeman or take them to the manager's office where he called them.

127

There was a crowd of women standing around the jewelry counter on the first floor one day when this young lad slipped some merchandise into his pocket and made for the side door. The floor walker saw him at the same time that I did so we both caught him at the same time, just outside the door. He said to the youth, "Son, you have some merchandise that you haven't paid for, and we are holding you for the police." A shriek went up from one of the women at the jewelry counter, yelling that someone had taken her billfold from her purse. The "floor walker" made for the disturbance. Holding the frail hand of the boy, I asked him where he was going to fence the stuff. His frightened voice told me that he only wanted a Christmas gift for his sick mother. Maybe it was because I didn't like the "floor walker," or maybe it was because I felt sorry for the lad. Anyway, I had the recovered merchandise and told him to beat it before the cops got there. I took the cheap jewelry, "costume," I think they call it, on back to the counter, and "old grouch" asked me where the little thief was. I told him that he got away. He cursed.

Christmas Eve was my last day of work on the temporary job, so I was mostly just strolling around the store. The toy department had an electric train going as I walked by, then there he was, just watching that train as it went through the tunnels and around and around. Then I saw the other one. The young culprit had a twin, and they were both looking long and wishfully as the train whistle sounded. My young friend saw me and started to shove off. I motioned for them to stay where they were and assured them that I would do them no harm as long as they left things alone.

Two hours later, passing back through the toys they were still there. We chatted a while, and I paid $1.50 for a train that you wind up and sent them home. Walking through the store, listening to the Christmas carols and watching the joyous look on people's faces made me feel good in spite of the hard times. On the way home I cursed myself for giving away my rent for another week.

The next time I saw the twins was at the bus station. One had coca cola caps fastened to the soles of his shoes, and the other one had spoons in his hands. The lids against the concrete and the spoons made such a rhythm that I wanted to dance. The cigar box near them had three nickels in it. I thought long and hard before I dipped into my pocket and threw in a quarter for the entertainment. The quarter was the admission to see Mae West in person at the Paramount. "What the hell?" I said to myself and went home.

The next day, which was Saturday, I was helping sweep out the Tabernacle when "Pete and Repeat" came by. They offered to help, and it was then that I learned the boys lived in one of those old dilapidated houses down Luckie Street just down the street from us. Their mother was ill and stayed in bed all the time. Their father left for the oil fields in Oklahoma to find work. Afterwards, a bundle of brooms was missing according to the man in charge of the cleaning, and he was calling the police. I told him to forget it and went looking for the twins. An hour later there they were next to the Hurt Building attempting to hawk the brooms for a dime a piece. The three of us took the brooms back to the church.

Later in the day, while strolling down Luckie Street, I saw where the boys lived. They were on the porch sobbing. I found their mother in a dirty bed coughing and gasping for breath. I ran to the First Methodist and found Dr. Harris in his study. He immediately dispatched someone to see about the boys' mother. She was carried to Grady Hospital. Four days later I met the boys coming up the sidewalk and told them that I had gone as far as I could go and was returning to the farm that afternoon. I only had bus fare left. The boys told me about Pierce Harris getting them a job caddying out at East Lake, and some women had cleaned up their house and brought them some food. That's the last time I ever heard from the twins.

This well dressed couple came to see me yesterday. There wasn't any doubt about it, they were class. The man asked me if I ever heard of twins nicknamed "Pete and Repeat." It was Pete from 1938, forty-three years ago. They had read something the other day which made them know about me. His wife told me that he often spoke of my friendship to two little waifs.

I was dumbfounded; here is Pete who lives in the most elite section of Atlanta, and Repeat is a missionary in Africa. Pete was a lawyer after the Korean conflict, and now was an executive with a large company. Morgan Black and Pierce Harris helped them when their mother died, "but it was you," he said, "that kept us from going bad, real bad."

The couple stayed about two hours. I was bubbling inside, and there was a funny feeling in my stomach. After they left I couldn't hold it in any longer. I went in the yard and yelled as loud as I could, "Whooee!" My wife came out and asked, "What on earth are you hollering about?" I didn't answer. I don't expect anybody to understand.

 ## One Day You'll Be Antique

I don't guess I should've been, but I was. I was startled by a young punk the other day when he called me "Pop." This makes a fellow kinda take a little more notice on how to know you are growing older.

Everything hurts and what doesn't hurt . . . doesn't work. You feel like the night before and you haven't been anywhere . . . . You get winded just playing checkers . . . . But, I suppose the worst thing of all is when you look, your children are looking middle aged.

Startled? Or maybe I was shocked until I started counting the things that make me know that I'm growing older, like when you join a health club and don't even go. And then when your mind makes all those contracts that your body can't keep, then you've about had it, I guess. I'm perfectly contented looking forward to a dull evening, something I never noticed before.

But, when you sit in a rocking chair and can't seem to get it going, it's about time for some Hadecol. I tried this and had the damnedest hangover the next day you ever heard of. And, when dialing long distance wears you out, it's time to quit cigarettes. All these things just add to the misery. When you sink your teeth into a steak and they stay there, then you know there is no turning back, and we have to make the best of it.

The word "Pop" makes me boil, but to be called this by a punk who isn't even kin to you just heats the pot more . . . . Then I was at a place the other night with some young folks and they kept calling me "Old Timer." Now that really hurts and startles one even more. All these things are proof that I'm growing older, but the last straw was that that little old grey-haired lady that I helped across the street just happened to be my wife.

Call me "pop," or call me "old timer," but we have something on the young folks. We don't have house notes. We don't have car payments. As a matter of fact, we don't have any kind of payments, so there. No sir, we don't have to lie awake at night wondering how we can send Junior to college either, but neither do we have to sweat out a certain time of the month to see how our wife is feeling. So I guess everything has its advantages, and I'm not about to sit down and wait for them to call me from "the home" and tell me they now have a room for me. I know full well how the only way a room becomes available at "the home."

Young folks just do not understand us and our old fashioned ways. For we gotta secret longing for the ole A Model days. We get a kind of comfort in this living in the past. We've learned as time goes onward, that youth and beauty cannot last.

Now a word to all you youngsters. About the pleasures that you seek. You may live and love the present, but one day, dammit, you'll be antique.

Play It Again, Sam

Play Me A Sad Song, Sam

People are just as happy as they make up their minds to be!

Didja ever notice that when a guy is sad or unhappy about something that he enjoys it?

Sure, when a feller loses his girl or has a fight with his wife, doesn't he go in a bar and play sad songs over and over while he cries in his beer, feeling sorry for himself? He never plays something to cheer him up . . . .

Women who like to be sad either do the same thing or tune in on a soap opera which would make anyone sad. Yes, they want to be sad and unhappy, but why? I can't understand why they don't tune in on a comedy or something, but it just has to be something sad.

Didja ever see someone who likes to go to funerals?

Yes, maybe partly out of respect, but some go to be sad. There are regular funeral goers who don't even know the deceased, but they will go to the church and cry.

There is a time when a person drinks to be happy, but he will lose this feeling after a while and want to be unhappy. Alcohol affects different people in different ways . . . . Some want to fight . . . some want to love . . . that is, before they have too many . . . and some just want to cry . . . .

Doctors tell us to get out of the environment where it is unpleasant, but no, a feller and most all women have to stick around and if it isn't sad enuff, they will find a place that is.

To have the blues at times is a natural thing, according to psychiatrists, but a person should try to overcome it by thinking of good things or changing locales and company quickly.

If something bothers you, do like the little boy in the first aid class. The instructor asked Scottie what he would do if he got his arm broken in three places?

Scottie thought a minute and replied, "I'd stay outta them places!"

Anyway, I remember when a man got the blues he would grab a train and ride. It was the woman who got the blues and hung her lil head and cried!

Aw, to heck with it! I'm leaving on a jet plane as quickly as I can get to the airport . . . meanwhile "Play Me A Sad Song, Sam!"

History Lesson For Today

When one takes the time to relate the ordinary to the ordinary, he can come up with some very unusual circumstances. Consider, for example, Presidents Lincoln and Kennedy.

Lincoln was elected in 1860 and Kennedy was elected in 1960. They were both concerned with civil rights. Both were slain on Friday and in the presence of their wives.

Their successors, both named Johnson, were Southerners and had served in the U.S. Senate. Andy Johnson was born in 1808 and Lyndon Johnson was born in 1908.

John Wilkes Booth and Lee Harvey Oswald were both murdered before trials were held. Booth was born in 1839 and Lee Harvey Oswald was born in 1939. Booth and Oswald were Southerners favoring radical ideas.

Both Kennedy's and Lincoln's wives lost children through death while living at the White House. President Lincoln's secretary was named Kennedy and warned him not to go to the theater. President Kennedy's secretary was named Lincoln and advised him not to go to Dallas.

President Kennedy was shot to death in a Lincoln, which was made by the Ford Motor Company. Lincoln was killed in the Ford Theater. The killers of both Booth and Oswald had the last name of Ruby.

I wonder if you knew that Benjamin Franklin claimed the bald eagle was too common to be made America's national symbol. Franklin instead favored the turkey.

I like history, including picking out a few other things that didn't get much attention in our history books.

One of the things that our history teachers failed to tell us is that when Martin Van Buren was vice president, he presided over the Senate wearing a pair of pistols. And in 1865, Confederate President Jefferson Davis offered to abolish slavery in the South in exchange for diplomatic recognition from England and France. The war ended before either country could respond.

It was Theodore Roosevelt who coined the phrase, "Good to the last drop," for Maxwell House. And did you know that from 1931 until the beginning of World War II, graduates to be of the Japanese Naval Academy were asked on their final exam, "How would you carry out a surprise attack on Pearl Harbor?"

Now for a few questions for the movie fans: What dance played a prevalent role in the movie *Can Can*? Name the songs made popular by the following movies: *Three Coins in a Fountain*, *Never on Sunday*, *Goldfinger*, and *The Way We Were*. And did you know that Cary Grant had an illustrous film career, but never won an Academy Award? Can you identify the films with these significant lines: "Hi, honey, guess who's coming to dinner?" and "We'd better go; it's almost midnight, cowboy."?

Just for fun, see how many of the following questions you can answer. What other group of four words besides "In God We Trust" appears on most U.S. coins? Does Lincoln wear a tie on the penny? What seven-letter word other than "America" appears on all U.S. coins (less than a dollar) issued after 1883? Does it say "post" or "postal" on the cards you mail? What letters do not appear on your telephone dial? Which two groups of the three letters on a typewriter are arranged in alphabetical order? Of the thirteen bars in the American flag, which are in the majority, the red or white? How many prongs does an ordinary fork have? The Statue of Liberty holds what in her left hand?

How many spade pips (suit markings) on the ace of spades? Which king in a standard pack of cards usually has no moustache? An inch on an ordinary ruler is usually divided into how many equal parts? And on what side does a policeman wear his badge?

Answers on the next page.

Answers to the quiz on the previous page:

"United States of America" appears on most U.S. coins along with "In God We Trust." Lincoln wears a bow tie on the penny. "Liberty" is the other seven-letter word which appears on most U.S. coins with "America." Postal, not post, appears on the cards we mail. The letters Q and Z do not appear on the telephone dial. F, G and H are in alphabetical order on the typewriter, also J, K and L. Seven red bars and six whites appear on the American flag. There are four prongs on most forks. The Statue of Liberty holds a book in her left hand. There are three suit markings on the ace of spades. The king of hearts doesn't have a moustache. There are sixteen divisions in an inch on rulers. Finally, a policeman wears his badge on the left side. What did you score?

And just for today: Don't be ashamed of the gray in your hair; think of the fun you had putting it there. One good thing about white hair is that you still have it. And did you ever notice, for every successful man, there is always that joker who knew him "when."

 Why A Five-Foot Deputy

It really happened in Pickens County a few years ago before marked police cars: a sheriff was running for re-election, and stopped in a remote section of the county. A woman came to the door, and the sheriff, with his hat in his hand, said, "Lady, I'm running for sheriff."

The woman quickly exclaimed, "We shore do need one!"

This same sheriff was about six feet, seven inches tall. His deputy might have been five feet if he stood on his tippy toes. The sheriff was asked why he had such a small deputy.

"When we go to arrest a drunk and he wants to fight, guess which one he jumps on," was the large sheriff's reply.

Of 'Tomater' And 'Dough'

A foreign visitor at the State Capitol recently observed that the governor and lieutenant governor of Georgia didn't talk like they came from the same country, much less the same state.

The visitor was talking about the governor's inability to use "r's" where they belong in his speech, while the lieutenant governor had the ability to use "r's" where they didn't belong.

North Georgia and south Georgia have often been confusing to out-of-state visitors because the two sections of the state are so different in looks and industry, as well is in speech.

Georgia history even shows that a difference of opinion arose about secession in 1860. It was soon after the adjournment of the Secession Convention that a startling fact became known all over the state: Pickens County was still flying the Union flag from the courthouse in Jasper, according to a reprint in the *Pickens County History* from the *Georgia History*.

The fact was noted that Pickens County had practically seceded from the Confederacy. Appeal after appeal was made to Governor Brown to send troops to cut down the Union flag. Brown declined to do this. Brown had served as judge of the Blue Ridge Circuit before he was elected as chief executive of the state. He knew the mountain people, being one of them. "They will take it down when they get good and ready," Brown was quoted as saying.

There were very few slaves in the county, and the citizens were flying the Union flag in protest of a war over slavery. The north Georgians didn't think it was their place to defend the rights of the south Georgia plantation owners to keep their slaves.

139

It has been recorded that the same men of Pickens County who were responsible for flying the Union flag took it down themselves after thirty days, and then went on to fight for the South. Many of these same Pickens Countians gave their lives during the Civil War.

Since that time, there have been many differences of opinion down at the statehouse by legislators who still feel that they are from different sides of the Mason-Dixie line.

Waleska, in Cherokee County, where Reinhart College is located, was really named "Warluski" according to Georia history. It seems that some of the south Georgia legislators thought the north Georgians were putting an "r" where it shouldn't be, like some did in "tomater" and potater." Papers at the State Capitol were changed by the south Georgians, removing the "r," hence the name of "Waleska" finally replaced "Warluski," the latter being the name of a chief's daughter who worked for Lewis Reinhart, founder of the college. It was said that Reinhart had so much love for his house maid that he named the town for her. Anyway, the south Georgians took the "r" clean out of the town.

So Lieutenant Governor Miller can say "tomater" and "potater" if he wants to, and Governer Busbee can say "flo" for floor and "dough" for door, and people will still get the message.

Tater Creek To Two-Egg

A while back, I wrote about the bridge located on the Tennes-see-Georgia line which carried the sign "Tater Creek" for many years. This was before a state highway crew came through and changed the sign to read "Potato Creek." The sign crew didn't know that the creek was named for a family, "Tater," and not the vegetable.

This piece brought mail from all across the country, and a telephone call from the Reader's Digest people. Most of the mail told of places with odd names and how they got them. There is Seroco, North Dakota, which got its name because folks in that area depended on the mail order house of Sears, Roebuck and Company for their needs.

There are seven two-letter word names of places in the United States, including Ed and Uz, both in Kentucky. According to other information, Likely, California, received its name when, in 1876, the natives sent three names to the Post Office Department and had them all rejected because they duplicated names of towns in that state. One man then said that it was not likely they would ever get a suitable name, and someone else then picked on the word not likely to have already been used as a name.

One of the most famous names in California is Modesto, according to Bonnie Newton. She says that when W. C. Ralston, a San Francisco financier, refused to have a town named for him, he was credited with modesty; and the place was named Modesto, meaning "modest," or "modest man."

In Mississippi, Old Why Not was established about three miles above the present Why Not. When trying to decide on a name, everyone would say "Why not call it . . . ." The official in Washington chose Why Not because every letter he received began with "Why not call it . . . so and so."

Unclear handwriting is the reason that Arab, Alabama, is called Arab, instead of Arad. The first postmaster in 1858 sent the name of his son to someone he knew in Washington, suggesting that the post office be called this. His son's name was Arad, and the postmaster just happened to make his "d's" backward.

Two Egg, Florida, is so named because about twice a year the settlement's only storekeeper had a hen that would lay two eggs in one day. A town in Maryland is named Accident because in 1774 some land was marked off "by accident." The world's shortest place names are not in the United States. One is the French of Y, and the Norwegian village of A, pronounced "Aw."

In Fannin County, Georgia, there is a place called Dry Branch. Nearby, Polk County, Tennessee, went them one better and named a place Extra Dry Branch. There was much mail suggesting that Waleska, Georgia, be changed back to Warluski, its original name, in honor of an Indian chief's daughter. South Georgians down at the state Capitol called the town Wah-lus-kuh, finally ending up with Waleska on state papers.

In northwest Pickens County, there is a place called Blaine. The place was first called Talking Rock until the coming of the railroad in 1884, and the town was moved three miles to be on the railroad. A post office was granted to the new settlement, but it needed a name. The hills were reeking with revenue officers who got their jobs under the Republican administration. James Blaine, the governor of Vermont, was the Republican nominee opposing the Democrat Grover Cleveland. The revenue agents, seeking favor of who they thought would be the next president, strong-armed the locals to call the new post office Blaine, after their party leader.

The agents were sent packing when Cleveland defeated Blaine, but the settlement still bears the name of the Republican Blaine. However, Pickens went for Blaine and has gone Republican in presidential elections since, with the exception of Roosevelt in 1932, and Jimmy Carter, who carried the county with the largest mandate of any presidential candidate, in 1976. Nearby Fannin County had never gone Democratic in the history of the county until native son Jimmy Carter carried it quite handily.

Are Speed Traps Gone?

A little piece in the paper the other day brought to mind just how much times have changed in the last few years. It was about a town down in South Georgia that didn't want their policeman busting anybody for doing a little speeding.

Before the thirties, a friend and I took a journey down through the flatlands of Georgia and on to Florida; quite an adventure back then for a couple of eighteen year olds. We had an old strip-down of a car which we had pieced together with hay baling wire, and were proud of the fact that we had worked on the carburetor until she would do fifty down a slanted place in the road.

This was the days when "fooling around" didn't have anything to do with sex. It just meant you didn't have a job. The Coca-Cola Company sponsored the Atlanta Crackers on the radio, and we called it "dog trotting" instead of "jogging." It was "the last straw," not the "bottom line," and it was called "shacking up" instead of "living in."

After four flat tires which we fixed on the fender and, of course, at the hottest point on the road, we came to this small town. We were chugging along at about fifteen miles an hour when this policeman pulled us over. The fellow didn't know how to talk without cussing as he told us we were doing forty in a twenty-five mile an hour zone. We tried to tell him that our old car would't do forty, but he was having none of that. "You're in a heapa trouble," he said, and he had me ride with him in the old, unmarked police car while my buddy drove in front of us to the City Hall, a little place that looked like an outhouse. I asked the policeman how he knew that we were doing forty since the speedometer wasn't working on his old coupe. He patted the big old gun in his holster, and I knew how he knew.

We got down to the place, and there wasn't anyone there, so the policeman handed me his ticket book and told me to fill it in, whereas we could pay him fifteen dollars and be on our way. I took a chance; I just knew he couldn't read and write. I wrote on the ticket in big letters, "YOU ARE A BIG BASTID!" I've often wondered what his partner said about that when they were splitting our cash.

A few times after the war, I was stopped in towns south of Atlanta. Once, the red light in a small town was hidden behind a big limb of a live oak tree, and to make doubly sure that it couldn't be seen by a driver, some of that south Georgia moss was placed in such a way, swinging from the tree, that the moss was all you could see. We had to cut our vacation short because of the fifty dollars of which the police relieved us for running a red light.

South Georgia was not the only place in our great state where tourists were picked instead of cotton. In my home town of Jasper, during the Big Depression, a car drove up in front of the court house and parked. A deputy sheriff was standing on the sidewalk. He gave a big spit of tobacco juice to the white side walls of the car, and asked the man where he was from. "I'm from Memphis," replied the stranger.

That deputy looked the stranger right in the eye and said, "What the heck you doing with that Tennessee tag on then?"

Georgia On My Mind

Rembering Mules And Ralph McGill

Ralph McGill reminds me of mules; or maybe it's the other way around, mules remind me of Ralph McGill. It may sound strange to some that mules would bring back the memory of such a great person as the former editor of *The Atlanta Constitution*, but the man had a thing about mules. He often would have his driver stop the car so he could get out and watch a farmer plowing one of the hybrid beasts. When he wrote a pretty stiff column, he would say, "You gotta put the hay down where the mules can reach it."

He once wrote a sad and understanding column about a farmer who drowned himself after his old mule died. "The mule was the social link," wrote McGill. "Without him, there could be no visiting on Sundays or the winter days when the crops were laid by. On a small Southern farm, the mule was the center of life."

The part I liked best was, "Matt Usher had only one mule. As others before him have done, he learned in his loneliness to talk to the mule as they worked together through the long days of plowing, of cultivating, of harvesting. And there was always communion, even though the mule was silent."

"A mule," he wrote, "has sense like a man. The horse is a silly fool which will run back into a burning barn because it is a symbol of safety. A mule will break down a door to get out. So it was in bygone days, before the boll weevil and the machines came, that men sang and talked to their mules in the fields, and there was companionship and mutual trust between them because a mule knows how to listen."

There was much more in McGill's column, but he told about Matt Usher's mule dying and how Matt Usher thought it over, and in his loneliness, wrote a note, weighted it down with a rock on the path, and walked down to the pond where he so often had taken his mule to drink. "My old mule is gone, I am drowned in this pond."

I know a lot about mules, and there is another man, Joshua Lee, who is now a professor at North Carolina State University, who has talked to a lot of mules. Josh grew up on a Georgia plantation during a time when people depended on mules to work the land and took pride in owning the hard-tailed animals. Lee wrote a book about this called, *With Their Ears Pricked Forward — Tales of Mules I've Known*, published by John F. Blair Co., Winston-Salem, North Carolina.

I know a little bit about everything Joshua is talking about. The names of his mules were the same as ours when I lived on a one-horse farm, or one-mule farm, whichever you prefer to call it. However, I can go Lee one better on just about everything he tells about, but I will have to give him credit for touching up my memory a little tad. Josh's father had mules named Mary, Rox, Belle, Pender Jane, Fox, and had teams like Minnie and Alice, and Mr. Clyde and Old Bill. At one time the elder Lee owned a mule that they called "Old Alec."

We had a mule when I lived on the farm called "Old Alec." I know a lot of folks who had a mule called Alec, and somehow it always worked around to "Old Alec." I never knew why "old" had to be a part of "Alec," but that's the way it was. Belle was another name that was hung on a mule that we owned. For the benefit of those who don't know, a female mule is called a mare mule and a male is called a horse mule.

One mule named Kate that we had when I was about 12 always tried to run me out of the barn or pasture when I approached her with a bridle. She would lay those ears back, bare her teeth and charge. She always stopped a few steps in front of me after she saw her bluff was gone. We would go for a bareback ride down to Talking Rock or across the mountain, and that mule seemed to like it better than I.

Old Kate is the only mule that I ever saw who would sit down like a dog, and at times try to scratch her ear with her hind hoof. It never quite reached, but Kate would go through the motion anyhow. We attributed this to the dog that followed her around in the pasture and in the field; and even when she went to town, that dog was right at her heels.

The reprint of Ralph McGill's columns, published by the Cherokee Publishers, Covington, and Joshua Lee's mule book are two books that I love.

Keeping Presidential Company

Being the guest of the son of the President of the United States is not much different from going somewhere with your neighbor, but that's because Jack Carter, the first son of President Jimmy Carter, wants it that way.

I drove over to Calhoun to meet Jack at his office to accompany him as a guest to visit the Georgia General Assembly on Valentine's Day by a prearranged talk. Jack and two secret service men drove up shortly after I arrived. I got in their station wagon, and I heard the driver say on his radio, "Smith, now leaving Calhoun for Atlanta." The person on the other end of the communications acknowledged.

Jack and I, riding in the back seat, talked all the way down like conversation was soon to go out of style. He doesn't want anyone to get the idea that he wants special privileges because he is the President's son, but this secret service business is the law.

We arrived at the state capitol about 10:00 a.m. and proceeded to the third floor where the law making bodies meet. One of the secret service men went with us and one stayed with the car. The latter is for communications back to Jack's home where his wife and 18-month-old son Jason were with their security agents.

We were welcomed by everyone. There was Rep. Joe Frank Harris, one of the most dedicated representatives in the state, leaving his seat to come speak to us. Senator Beverly Langford, father-in-law of Jack's, did the same. Many other representatives came to see us that I hadn't seen in a long time.

Of course the secret service man, Carl Smith, who is from a small town in Maine, was right with us making sure that no one got between him and us. At first I thought his job was for Jack's security only, but soon learned that he considered me his responsibility also, since I was Jack's guest. Smith carried a small radio on his person with which he kept in constant contact with his partner back in the station wagon.

Carl Smith is in charge of what is known as the Calhoun detail. Leonard Egan from Ohio is just on temporary assignment for which there will be a permanent assignment for a team later.

A mobile home unit is set up in the Carter lot as an office for the secret service with a blind between it and the street. Carl told me they checked with the neighbors to make sure that it was all right, which it was, and often the neighbors bring them home-made cookies and other goodies.

I was impressed by the way Carl Smith and Leonard Egan did their jobs. These men go through rigid training from two to four years before being given this kind of responsibility. Smith, who accompanied us wherever we went, is built like a wrestler, walks with the smoothness of a cat and seems ready to spring at any minute. Observing his manner, I concluded that although he is armed, he is ready to jump between his responsibility to protect them from anything. They lay their lives on the line for their job. There are times when the security man will appear like a sleeping alligator, but if someone comes close, his eyes begin to dance and he is ready for anything.

Joe Cummings, chief of *Newsweek* magazine, invited us to lunch which we accepted over at the swanky Commerce Room. We enjoyed two hours of conversation and a delightful meal before shaking hands with Jack Tarver, the president of Atlanta papers and Hal Gulliver, editor of *The Atlanta Constitution*. Of course Smith the bodyguard ate with us while Egan stayed with the car.

We went back to the capitol where Celestine Sibley came out to greet us, and then over to the Omni where I had never been. This is some place, but a lot of walking for a 57-year-old man keeping up with a 30-year-old boy, but Jack made it clear this was my day and he let me set the pace. He bought his wife Judy roses for Valentine's Day, then we went to Georgia Industry and Trade which is located in the building.

At 5:30 Carl Smith spoke into his radio to Egan and told him to bring the car around front. We got in and I heard Smith say, "Leaving Atlanta for Calhoun." A girl's voice acknowledged. Probably Carl's wife, since she is moving here.

A lot of conversation between Jack and me on the way home, but both of us began to tire. I shook hands with the guys who had been protecting us, then I shook hands with Jack as he told me,

"You'll soon get an invitation to a steak dinner in the White House. Are you going?"

"You're mighty right," I replied. I have a strong feeling that the Carters never forget a friend, and somehow I get the feeling that they never forget an enemy.

Jack is not running for any political office any time soon, and he has put aside his law practice to give full time to his grain elevator that he is now building in Calhoun. He has the welfare of the state of Georgia at heart. He is the trustee of Dalton Junior College and a family man. Like my wife, he comes from south Georgia, but you would think that he is the son of a mountain moonshiner instead of the President of the United States.

 ## Meet Jimmy, Not Jim

Will the real Jimmy Townsend please stand up? I'm not the Jim Townsend who is the former editor of the *Atlanta Magazine*. (He died in April 1981.) I'm Jimmy Townsend. The Jim Townsend, who held the job of associate editor of *The Atlanta Weekly* that comes with the Sunday Atlanta papers, was an educated writer. He held degrees in journalism and held some big jobs with daily papers around the South. He was a good writer and capable of using the "fifty dollar words," as we say up here in the mountains.

I'm Jimmy Townsend, the man who never went to college a day in my life, but you can find me some Saturdays in a football stadium yelling my head off. I got most of my education by reading *The Market Bulletin* and *The Country Gentleman*. What you read is for real. I have never tried to pretend, and I've never tried to appear to be something that I am not.

The Jim Townsend who wrote the book *Dear Heart* is not related to me. I met him for the first time one day when I walked into his office down at the *Atlanta Journal* and said, "I'm Jimmy Townsend." He replied, "I'm Jim Townsend," and that was it. Jim Minter, the executive news editor, wanted him and what Minter wants around here, Minter gets.

I haven't read *Dear Heart*, but I have read some of Jim Townsend's work in *Brown's Guide* and I know the book will be interesting. I hope that this chapter will straighten things out for Atlanta's Jim Townsend, because he was just too good to be confused with an old mountain man like myself.

I receive books all the time from highly educated writers for me to review. I reviewed a book once and forgot to mention the name of the publisher, and I promptly got a call from a rough-talking man from New York.

"How cum," he roared, "you didn't mention the name of our company in your review?"

"Hell," I replied, "I didn't know that you wanted to sell the company. I thought you wanted to sell the book."

I get a lot of questions about how to become a writer. Well, first you have to have an opportuntiy. Talent isn't worth a darn without it. And a writer writes because he has something to say, and not just because he wants to say something.

If you've read my other book, *Mountain Echoes*, then you know that my vocabulary is about the size of a mustard seed. I have enjoyed the things that happen to an author after a book is completed. Nobody seemed to mind that my sentence construction is a little bad, nor do they seem to mind that I didn't hunt up any college words just to please a few folks.

Writing a book was an adventure. To begin with, it was a toy, an amusement; then it became a mistress, and then a master, and then a tyrant.

He Served More With Dignity
Than Anyone Else

Excusing funerals, I have cried twice in my adult life. Once when Jimmy and Rosalynn Carter walked down Pennsylvania Avenue on Inauguration Day in Janurary 1977. I had an invitation to the great event but elected to stay at home and watch the ceremonies on TV. I was sitting there in front of the fireplace just staring into the wood fire waiting anxiously for the thing to begin when I began thinking. At my age I don't know whether thinking is good for a fellow or not.

My mind drifted back to the Army days during World War II. Most of us here in the mountains rarely left them. It was very seldom that we even got down to Atlanta 65 miles away.

We knew about the Civil War because we had studied all about "Bull Run" and "The Battle of Atlanta" in school. Besides that, as we were growing up there were a few veterans from this foolish conflict still around. Some of them wouldn't wear overalls because they were blue.

When the draft started in 1940, it paved the way for us Southerners to mix with Northerners. There isn't any use of my attempting to be polite, we were rebels and they were yankees. Erskin Caldwell's books were hot and the boys from the other side of the Mason-Dixon actually believed that the contents of these paperbacks were true of every girl in the South. There was many a black eye caused by us defending the honor of our Southern women.

These were the days of Gene Talmadge and his red galluses. Everybody both here and abroad had heard of Talmadge and his policies of keeping blacks out of schools, and in most cases keeping the blacks from voting. Gene did a lot of cutting up to prove his points, and even though he embarrassed boys from Georgia he only added fuel to the fire for the Northern boys.

Herman Talmadge came along after the war and kept within his father's policies most of the time. Then Lester Maddox made it difficult for us to travel with our families. The Georgia tags on our cars were a dead giveaway for some blacks to get behind us and instead of passing, just set down on his horn for several blocks and sometimes miles. They seemed to be saying, "We're in charge up here. Go back where you came from."

I suppose that it was how people from the other part of the nation felt about folks from Georgia that made me so anxious to see Jimmy Carter elected President of the United States. A Georgian, I thought, in the White House, will put a little more polish on the people from the land of Cotton. I was watching as Jimmy and Rosalynn began their walk from the capitol to the White House when the darndest feeling came over me that I had ever witnessed. Tingling was running up and down my spine and I began to cry. My wife came home about that time and asked, "What on earth is the matter?" I said, "I can't help it, Mama, it's taken us 200 years, but by golly we're in charge now."

Jimmy Carter proved to be a gentleman and a credit for Georgia just like I had hoped. Some things for us began to change with everybody it seemed, but the Eastern press. These fellows still had the same attitude that the boys from Brooklyn had during World War II.

Right away the President and the First Lady invited Geri and me to a state dinner at the White House. I was a little nervous about this because I had never worn a tuxedo in my life. My wife wanted to go so we went down to Rich's and rented not only the black tie outfit, but a pair of shining shoes to boot. The dinner was in honor of the Chancelor of Germany, Helmut Schmidt and Mrs. Schmidt.

Rosalynn Carter was looking after us pretty well and, of course, Mrs. Schmidt was with her most of the time. I'll have to admit that my white hair and the black dinner outfit looked pretty good on me. So good, in fact, that a reporter asked which senator I was. Mrs. Schmidt remarked how nice the tux looked with my hair, and so expensive looking, too. "It only cost twelve dollars," I replied. "You're kidding!" she exclaimed. "No ma'am, I'm not, but that's only for one night." She laughed.

I didn't try to put on any airs. I was just myself. I saw some fellows there from the North who got into some embarrassing situations trying to be something that they were not. The butlers came around with little trays filled with glasses of wine. I reached to get a glass when my wife, knowing that I can't drink, elbowed me in the stomach. "Why can't I have a glass of wine like everybody else?" I asked.

"Because," she said, "it wouldn't be five minutes until you would be calling the Chancelor of Germany a 'damn kraut.' That's why you can't have any wine."

When Mrs. Schmidt got back to Germany she wrote us a letter. She wanted us to visit them for a few days. She obviously didn't like "put-ons" either. We declined, however, and I've always felt that my wife feared that I might slip around and get a glass of wine and cause us a little trouble in that country.

* * *

When Jimmy Carter was running for President I prayed. I told the Lord that I wasn't one of those fellows who was bothering him all the time, so if he could help us out I would appreciate it.

After the state dinner, I thought that this would be my last trip to Washington, which proved to be incorrect. In June 1979 the President invited my family and me to spend the weekend in the White House. My son-in-law, Doug Vaughan, my daughter Tracy, our only grandson Chris, my wife Geri, and I went back to the capitol city. The details of this trip are told in my book *Mountain Echoes*, so I will skip over our stay there.

We were to leave the White House on Monday, so I paid a little visit to the business end of the President's House. Walking down the hall I met Vice-President Mondale. He knew who I was. Everybody knows who spends the night in the White House. He offered his hand and asked politely, "How're things down South?". . . . Well, I knew who he was but I couldn't think what to call him, so I answered, "Just fine, your honor."

We left the White House Monday afternoon, as scheduled, to go to Williamsburg, Virginia. Gasoline was a little hard to find, but we stopped at a country store where the man putting gas in the car noticed our Georgia tag. Chris, my six-year-old grandson, had gone inside the store for a soft drink, a habit of his. I went to pay the man and saw that the proprietor was ribbing Chris. "Do you know Jimmy Carter?" he asked. "If you're from Georgia," he chided, "you should know the President."

Chris answered, "We spent the night in the White House last night." The man scoffed disbelievingly, "You mean you spent the night in the city where the White House is. Ain't that the truth now, son? The booger man will get little boys who tell stories."

I spoke up and said rather abruptly, "My grandson is telling you the truth. We slept at the White House last night." The man shut up, but as we went out the door I heard him tell his wife and the loafers standing around, "That old fool said they stayed all night in the White House," and they all roared with laughter.

We got to the city limits of Williamsburg where Doug, who was driving, stopped behind a car that was stopped for a red light. The car in front of us had a bumper sticker which read, "Honk Your Horn If You Love Jesus." Doug gave a little toot on the horn. A girl stuck her head out the window and yelled, "What's the matter? Can't you see the damn light's red?"

My family took the bus tour of the historic town, but I stayed around the Welcome Center to rest. I watched cars from all over the nation come and go. The faces beamed with pride and patriotism. I smiled. I felt good. My Americanism was showing all over me. I never thought about it, but Chris had never ridden a bus, so he was sitting as close to the bus driver as he could when they returned four hours later. He had on a little Tri-corn hat that made him look like a regular little revolutionary.

We stayed the night in Williamsberg and drove on home the next day. As we drove in Chris' driveway, his little playmate came running over to greet him. I expected Chris to start telling about staying in the White House, but he didn't. He exclaimed gleefully, "I got to ride a bus!"

Never in the history of this nation has a man served with as much dignity as Jimmy Carter. Never has any man represented these United States as has he in the way of morals. His determination to keep us out of war was frustrating, I'm sure, but he managed it with everything as explosive as it is in the world. He served this country with such dignity that I wish the Army would draft me and send me to Fort Slocum, New York, so I could get even with them yankees from World War II.

I never believed the polls. I just couldn't see such a loyal man as Jimmy Carter being turned down by the voters. But, the way things are in this world today, I doubt if any man, no matter how great, could ever be reelected to the top job. His forty-five million votes are nothing to be ashamed of. Yet, when he came on television to concede his defeat, I wept unashamed. I cried out loud as Ray Charles began singing, *Georgia, Georgia, Georgia On My Mind*.

The Music Goes Round And Round

If War Comes

The hounds of war are baying, there is no question about this. Slowly, achingly, like a fuzzy-cheeked boy from the country being lured by a city prostitute, the American people are being drawn toward an acceptance of the necessity of war.

And like biological changes that have changed the boy, world events since November 4 have transformed the American people. In a sense, the storming of the U.S. Embassy in Tehran and the taking hostage of the diplomatic personnel, there was itself an act of war.

It started a chain reaction of events that has led to where we are today, on the brink of a confrontation that could indeed be the war to end all wars — by destroying the world as we know it.

There are some things worth dying for, I suppose, and none should shirk his duty when the guns begin to shoot.

I have supported implementing the registration system for the draft, so the United States can be prepared to fight if that awful day comes. I think the American people generally support these moves, too. But let us all know, before the shooting starts, the horrible costs that war would bring.

What bothers me most, in all the war-talk, is that the people of this country don't know what war is. Not since the Civil War, which tore the guts right out of this country, have Americans seen war for what it is. The Auschwitzes and the My Lais have been considered horrors that are hard to believe, when in fact — in greater or in lesser measure — they are perfect examples of what war is all about.

161

Something else bothers me about the drift toward war this nation has been taking in recent months. It's that old men are making the decisions that the young men will die for. It has always been this way, and I guess always will be. But I still have to wonder if the drafting started in the Congress here, and the Parliment or whatnot of the Supreme Soviet, just how much stomach there would be for war. Not much, I suspect. The call to arms always is most stirring to those who don't have to do the dying.

We World War II veterans often think that young folks today are not patriotic, that they are cowards, when in a sense they have more guts than we ever had. When our war started we were in a deep Depression, no jobs, couldn't afford college so what the hell?

Today the young people have everything. A whole life that can be turned any way they want it. But college students for the most are willing to go right along with war because they know that America is the only country in the world where you can have a $70,000 mortgage and still be called a homeowner.

The Persian Gulf region is so important to the future of this country that Americans must militarily, if necessary, prevent its takeover by Russia. Everyone hopes, of course, the threat of war will die down, but we also know whenever people, or countries, make threats that they must be prepared to carry them out. . . . And that's why I support a registration system for the draft. If the Soviets back down, we all claim victory. If they call our bluff about the Persian Gulf, we must be ready to share in the consequences.

So let us go now, and prepare for war. But let us never forget that we are talking about preparing for hell on earth; for that time when there shall be weeping and gnashing of teeth.

Curing Inflation Is Easy

Now that we are in the third month of a new decade, we have the problems that arose from the seventies. Inflation, recession, unemployment, record interest rates to name a few. Gas is more than a dollar a gallon and heading for two; chilling home heating bills, increasing fuel imports and dwindling domestic resources are a few more increasing problems.

We have illiterate high school graduates and college grads who can't read. There are increasing numbers of unmarried mothers, which means that there have to be more unwed fathers out there somewhere. Adolescent alcoholics and preteen criminals keep our society at a low level.

Now everybody has compiled a list like this of what happened to us in the seventies, but everybody washed their hands, then wrung them out, hoping each new problem would go away and leave us alone. None of them did; none ever will. And if the eighties retain that attitude, the predicament will only get worse until someday, when we flat run out of energy and money and time, we will lose our way of life.

We have read over and over what the experts say, those who are paid to know the answers in psychology, energy, finance, politics, religion and education. Yet nobody has been very successful, at least so far, in convincing the American people what our problems are, much less give a cure for them.

This old country boy from the north Georgia mountains with a limited education in everything but experience is today trying his hand at solving our problems.

Our only alternative to "someday" is to cut back, slow down, take a deep breath and admit what the seventies were trying to tell us. America has limits. The innocent life we enjoyed from the late forties through the early sixties is gone forever. There is no more "happily ever after." There never was, so listen to what I have to say today and let me know if I do any worse than some of those high-paid guys and dolls.

Okay, so what can we do? Where do we start? By looking at the seventies, believe it or not; by looking past the mistakes and confusion, to salvage the lessons. Many are hidden, but they're there. Even the darkest days of the murky past ten years — Kent State, Watergate, Jonestown, Iran — taught us at least one good thing: that we could survive them.

Where America wants to be ten years from now is no secret. We want to be on the other side of the energy shortage and inflation. To reverse the energy outlook we must unite and conserve. If we don't we'll run out of gas. You say that you already knew that! Well, dammit, do it, it's that simple. We refused to conserve voluntarily, so fortunately our greedy demand for energy is making it so expensive we are forcing ourselves to conserve.

Already Americans are insulating and turning down thermostats to pinch pennies. We may get to washing dishes in the sink and drying our clothes on the clotheslines, but don't forget, we forced ourselves into this situation by refusing the President's request to conserve voluntarily. But this won't be so bad, we may get a World War II type kick out of working and succeeding together, as a country.

To cap inflation, we must stop spending and start saving. And I mean everybody, not just a few. Hide your charge cards. The buy-now-pay-later philosophy of the seventies created excess money and thereby diminished its value. The government needs to eliminate the debt it accumulated in the seventies, and there is a movement afloat to do this. A constitutional amendment that would guarantee a balanced budget. Don't laugh at me here, people laughed at Proposition 13, too.

Today folks are looking for someone or something to hold on-to. In fact they have become so desperate that they pick the first fast talker to offer himself. Jonestown was born this way. But at the same time, fire-and-brimstone evangelists and no-nonsense churches are becoming more popular, which will probably be good for all of us during the eighties.

Education's challenge for the eighties is to treat the kids' casualties. Those who got caught in the adult wave of do-it-if-it-feels-good morality and give-me-more-drugs; those who live with Mommy one week and Daddy the next; those whose parents have been busy at who-knows-what. All educators will have to be trained to be sensitive to these things and then it maybe can be helped.

Above all, Johnny and Janie are going to have to learn to read. They will have to learn period. Teachers will have to demand more from children, less electronic gadgets and more on basics, but we've got to do it.

Coping without charge cards, air conditioning, long-distance vacations and the like is difficult, but you'll get used to it. We never even had them and it ain't all that bad.

We like to think that it isn't fair to allow the price of gas to go so high. It is the $12,000-$25,000 group that causes inflation. Not the rich folks. There are more of us than there are of them. We are the ones who have four or five cars in our yard. We are the ones who send each of our children to school in a separate car. We are the ones who catch a plane to California just because we can charge it. We are the ones who keep the credit departments busy at the department stores. We are the ones who can kill inflation. Destroy your credit cards and inflation will be destroyed the next day.

You say that I'm not qualified to make these announcements. Heck! You don't have to be a cook to know when the food is bad. Anyway, all an economist is is someone who doesn't have any money who tells those who have it what to do with it.

It's Still Just Plain Gambling

Pari-mutual is nothing more than an euphemism for betting on horses. This substitute word for something unpleasant has come alive down at the state capitol. Most of us here in the mountains were raised thinking that gambling was one of the "no-no" Ten Commandments, but as we grew older we learned that "Thou shalt not gamble" is not even in the Bible. There have been thousands of laws passed simply trying to enforce the Ten Commandments. As a matter of fact, about all laws passed during the last 2,000 years were for this purpose. Gambling just doesn't happen to fall into this category.

Several years ago I was in Las Vegas doing what everybody else does in Las Vegas. I spotted a sign in one of the casinos which read, "$100,000 reward will be paid to the person who can show us where it says in the Bible that it is a sin to gamble." I just knew that the reward was the same as in my pockets, but, returning to my room at the hotel where there was a Bible handy, I thumbed through without success. Upon returning home I nearly wore the Bible out trying to win that reward, but with no success here either.

I wrote to Billy Graham, asking him what it said in the Holy Book about all this. He answered the question in his syndicated newspaper column by saying that the Bible does not exactly contain the words that it is a sin to gamble, but on the other hand he gave a number of reasons why gambling is wrong.

Like most fellows who have ever been in the armed services, poker playing and other games of chance became a little habit. When we left the service, Friday night poker games became routine, and some big-time gambling was done. I considered myself to be quite good at the skill of five card stud, playing any time there was a seat open.

It was in 1948 that I decided to borrow and invest everything that I could lay my hands on in the Little World Series of Poker in Phoenix City, Alabama. This was when the city on the other side of the river from Columbus, Georgia was known as "Sin City," and for good reason, too.

The game began as what was known in poker circles as a $10,000 take out. There are five players with each putting this amount on money before him. A player is eliminated when he loses his table stakes: thus, the last player left would become champion and $40,000 richer.

This is not a lot of money now, but in those days you could retire and live in luxury for the rest of your life on $50,000.

A few hands were dealt with everybody playing tight poker with no one losing or winning much. Cards were dealt again and I turned up the corner of my hole card just enough to see an ace. Top cards were dealt and my top card was an ace. I bet conservatively on my pair of aces, hoping to keep everybody in. They stayed, and with each card the betting got higher.

When fifth street was dealt and my aces backed were still high, I felt a relief because the highest card against me was a king that was showing. "A lock at the board," I thought as all of our money was now in the pot. I knew that one man had a pair of kings by the way he bet. He must have felt, too, that I had aces because everybody was getting up from the table when I said, "A pair of aces." The players still didn't notice until I almost screamed, "My gosh! That four looked like an ace!" The men looked and knew that I had misread my hand and the fellow with the pair of kings raked in the pot.

I fooled around with cards for a few years after that before quitting the game for good. It is my opinion that morality cannot be legislated. Each person has to find out these things for himself. LUCK IS ALWAYS AGAINST THE PERSON WHO DEPENDS ON IT.

I don't care what they do about "pari-mutual," but anybody who bets on the horses is a fool, and it would be my guess that the city of Atlanta would go broke in the business anyway. Look how they dabble into the pots of the other city enterprises.

Gamblers are superstitious fools. I was in Las Vegas when a man playing roulette seemed to hear a phantom voice say, "Bet it all on red." The man, thinking he had a super power behind him, did and won. "Bet it all on black," the voice whispered. He did and won again. "One more time on the black," came again. The gambler did and lost. . . . "Damn," said the voice as it faded away.

Pharmacists Make Good Politicians

It seems that every small town has a pharmacist that they like to talk about, according to our mail lately. A politician (who says that if we use his story to be sure and spell his name right) gives some good advice. Johan Aleimite of South Dakota says that when you are running for office, try to get the small town druggist on your side. "They have much more influence in their community than preachers." He (I don't want to spell that name again) reminds us of probably the best-known pharmacist in recent years, Hubert Humphrey, who worked in his father's drug store in his home town of Huron, South Dakota. HHH kept his pharmacist's license until he died.

Other Americans who at one time practiced pharmacy include Benjamin Franklin, Benedict Arnold and William Sidney Porter, who was a druggist in North Carolina before giving it up to write short stories under the pen name of O. Henry. Sir Isaac Newton of England and Johann Wolfgang von Goethe of Germany were two other pharmacists who went on to other things.

The first drug store opened in 754 A.D., according to *Stories about Everyday Things*. The store was in Bagdad and offered a wide range of medicine for that day. Camphor, cloves and many alcoholic preparations were sold. The store even had fruit syrups which led to the soda fountain many years later.

Well into the 19th Century, drug stores were dark, forbidden-looking places, lined with jars bearing Latin labels. But in 1825, Elias Durand of Philadelphia put in the first soda fountain in a drug store. It soon became something of a day care center for teenagers. Prohibition curtailed the hangouts in bars and cafes, and the drug store with a friendly druggist fast became the gathering place for everybody.

By 1929, 80 percent of America's 60,000 drug stores had installed a soda fountain. This declined by 1970 to about 12,000 drug stores because of various reasons, one being the competition of ice cream parlors and drive-ins; another that the stores needed the space for cosmetics and the like which are much more profitable.

The nature of drug stores has changed, too. Although most drug stores still keep a mortar and pestle lying around somewhere, as well as scales, 99 percent of all prescriptions require the pharmacist to do no more than take some capsules or tablets out of one bottle, put them in another bottle, and type up a label for it. What he does with the other twenty or thirty minutes you have to wait remains one of life's dark mysteries.

When we travel around the state, we find that there are still some of the old-fashioned drug stores in north Georgia. Some of them still have the friendly druggist that politicians seek out. Some still have soda fountains and even serve sandwiches. Reminds us of the sign in a drug store which reads: "Our Sandwiches are Made by a Licensed Pharmacist.". . . Another sign reads: "Try Our Cough Syrup; You Won't Get Any Better."

And then the story about a pharmacist who had just died — one of his colleagues told another, "Jack will be missed." "Yes," replied the other, "He knew just the right amount of salt to put on a chicken salad sandwich."

The old druggist and the old country doctor are fading from the American scene, but there are two Dean boys at Woodstock, Georgia, who won't give up. Their ages are 90 and 92, and they still go to the store every day. Nothing in the store now but Coca-Colas, which they refer to as "dopes," but they open the old drug store promptly at eight o'clock, close for lunch at twelve, and are right back on the job at one, where they remain until six o'clock. The Dean boys are uncles of Dean Rusk, which is probably where the former Secretary of State got his name and his stubbornness.

Americans Are Still Americans, No Matter

I get a feeling of nausea whenever I hear the ethnic word "wop" used. The word actually came from an act of U.S. Immigration officials stamping "W.O.P." on the identification papers of illegal aliens. The initials simply meant "without passport," but later became an ugly word. But to me, a man becomes an American when he is an American, no matter what.

I despise all ethnic words. The word "ethnic," according to Webster's, means "relating to races or large groups of people classed according to common traits and customs." Using this definition, all Southerners, and particularly Georgians, are an ethnic group.

One only has to read certain newspapers to know this to be true. Since Jimmy Carter was elected President, certain newspapers have made fun of the way we talk as well as many of our culture's customs. And then day in and day out these same papers come down hard on the President, not only on the front page, but often their editorial pages are filled with unjust criticism of the President. Some of the columnists even like to suggest that a Georgian is not competent to serve as President.

If Ted Kennedy, or anyone else from above the Mason-Dixon line, had accomplished what Carter has in the way of peace for the world, there is little doubt in my mind that the Northerner would be labeled as the best leader of all times by those newspapers. Likewise, if Jerry Ford had tackled the problems Carter has, he would be proclaimed another Abe Lincoln.

But no, not a Southerner. We are just an ethnic group to certain newspapers. We are characters straight out of an Erskine Caldwell novel. We have "little brains" and our women are "spicy little things that can't talk plain."

Just the other day, a lady commentator was talking about getting off a plane. You don't get off a plane, you get out of it. A male commentator was talking about getting on a train. You don't get on a train, you also get in it. These same people make fun of our "you all" but find nothing wrong with saying "youze" and "yez guys."

If a convicted man who voted for Jimmy Carter is mentioned in these newspapers, all at once the criminal becomes a "long-time bosom buddy of the President," even though Carter has never heard of the person. And Jimmy Carter is the first to admit there have been some mistakes made, but thank goodness no major ones.

Really, Carter's major mistake to Jack Anderson and some other writers is being born in Georgia. I don't know about "you all" but I'm damn tired of it myself. And if you're a Republican, it makes no difference, because you belong to the same ethnic group as Jimmy Carter because you live in Georgia.

It kinda reminds me of when I was a visitor at the White House last year. I was standing in the Oval Office with this secret service man staring at my "all overs," making me a little nervous. I thought I could fix things and so I exclaimed proudly, "I'm from Georgia!"

I may have imagined it, but I do believe the fellow looked down to see if I was wearing shoes.

Those Death Bed Changes

Luke McCoy has been around these mountains now for some 73 years. He was born to Amanda and Zekiel McCoy in the year of our Lord 1907.

The Rev. Zeke was a "hell fire and brimstone" preacher who traveled to mountain churches for many years, riding on a mule's back. The preacher was ambushed when Luke was about 15 years old, and he lay in a coma for four days before he died of gunshot wounds.

The killers were never arrested, but most folks speculated as to how it was the whisky people who killed the Rev. Zekiel McCoy. He had been warned before by moonshiners for preaching against the sin of drinking.

Luke was asked the other day if he believed in "death bed religion." Luke told them that he believed in any kind of religion, but went on to tell how his father, the Rev. Zeke, had felt about it. It seems that the preacher had been sent for on many occasions when someone was dying. The preacher and the person's family would pray for the dying one, sometimes all night, or until somebody thought the person was saved.

Sometimes the dying person would have lived a sin right up until he got sick. Many times the person had lived such a wicked life that even the devil didn't want him. But when the person was saved with a preacher present, whether it be on a death bed or not, the family was relieved. Now they would meet the sinner in heaven no matter what the dying person had done before.

172

"But there was a knuckle burr in all this," Luke said. "Sometimes the person who was supposed to die didn't. He got well; according to Paw, he always went back to his sinful ways." Luke said that his dad said that most of the time. The recovered sick man would be ten times worse than he had been before.

This conversation took place over at the court house the other day when somebody was talking about Ronald Reagan's "death bed conversion" on a lot of things when he became a candidate for President.

Reagan opposed the minimum wage law. Folks around here would still be making 20 cents an hour if it weren't for this law. Until recently, the Republicans' choice has wanted Social Security to be voluntary, which would kill it. Reagan has opposed for many years now any health plans for the poor.

He has been against welfare and the government financing of nursing care homes. There are many other programs that have helped people survive here in the mountains that Reagan opposed; but now he says he was just kidding.

I'm like Luke; I'm afraid of Reagan's "death bed religion" for fear that he might get well and then be ten times worse on the underprivileged.

In 1976, President Gerald Ford said over and over, Ronald Reagan can't start a war now, but he could if he were President. Now it seems that all Republican politicians have gotten a "death bed conversion" by saying they didn't mean it at all. I'm with Luke; I'm afraid of these people who have preached something for years, and all at once say they were just kidding.

Luke and I think that we could do a lot worse than Jimmy Carter.

Mountain Echoes

Mountain Echoes

My first book, entitled *Mountain Echoes* and published by Peachtree Publishers of Atlanta, Georgia, had around 200 or so of these quips I've been fooling around with for about fifty years now. Quips are one- or two-liners that may have a bit of truth or a little satire or be whimsical or just plain funny.

I've collected over five thousand of them and many have been published as *Mountain Echoes* in newspaper columns I have written for many years.

I've gotten so many letters about them from my first book that it only seems fair to share a few more with you:

Life is full of sunshine, but the stuff you step in is called experience.

We spend the first half of our lives trying to understand the older generation, and the second half trying to understand the younger generation.

If you want to be a failure, just try to please everybody.

The kindness we mean to show tomorrow cures no heart aches today.

Very few can stand the strain of being educated without feeling superior over it.

There are two sides to every question. . .if you don't have a stake in it.

Ignorance is when you don't know something and somebody finds it out.

177

It's more important to get where you're going than to get there quickly.

It's doggone hard to keep your temper when you know you're wrong.

Chewing gum proves that you can have motion without progress.

There is never time to do it right, but there is always enough time to do it over.

Bores have at least one virtue: they don't talk about other people.

Jealousy builds more fine homes than ambition.

The trouble with being a good sport is that you have to lose to prove it.

Measure a man by his integrity and not his profession.

The best substitute for brains is silence.

If winning ain't important, why do they keep score?

"Riding the fence" will get you in trouble with both sides. Even an umpire has half the crowd on his side, no matter how he calls the play.

It ain't no use putting up your umbrella until it rains.

If you drop the ball, don't gripe about the way it bounces.

Average is when you're no farther from the top than you are the bottom.

If men had no faith in one another, all of us would have to live within our incomes.

Remember money isn't everything, but also remember to make a lot of it before talking such foolish nonsense.

If you want some time to yourself, just be punctual.

There isn't anything that will make you forget your troubles like a pair of tight shoes.

Luck is a mighty unreliable thing to depend on.

Nothing makes one a better listener than hearing his name mentioned.

You can't achieve anything without getting in someone's way.

To be successful in a business or profession you must be wise enough to know that there is more corn than cement in America.

Tact is when you make guests feel at home even though you wish they were.

The best get-well cards are "four aces."

If you understand the other fellow's problem, then you have it half solved.

A lot of pessimists get that way by financing optimists.

Wisdom is the ability to separate courage from stupidity.

When you help someone up the hill, you are closer to the top yourself.

There is one thing worse than being talked about, and that is *not* being talked about.

Be moderate in all things. . .including moderation.

There is a difference between keeping your chin up and sticking your neck out.

It's always best to speak the truth unless you're a real good liar.

There is no lesser of two evils. Evil is evil.

When choosing between two evils, choose the one you haven't tried before.

There's nothing wrong with being mediocre as long as you're good at it.

When you try to make an impression, that's the impression you make.

If you don't pay back you'll soon be cured of the borrowing habit.

There is no such thing as "a little trouble" if you're the one that's in it.

Triple our problems many times over, and we'd still be better off than any other people on earth.

News is the same old thing, just happening to different people.

There's a difference between good sound reasons and reasons that sound good.

Breeding is the quality that enables a person to wait in well-mannered silence while the loudmouth gets the service.

Silence may be golden, but there are times when it's yellow.

Too much of this world is run on the theory that you don't need road manners if you drive a five-ton truck.

You can't plow a field by turning it over in your mind.

You can't make a comeback if you haven't been anywhere.

To protect your teeth, see your dentist twice a year — and mind your own business.

If you think that the Bible should be updated, just remember that there hasn't been a new sin in 5000 years.

The Brooklyn Zoo has a sign in a building which reads: "THIS ANIMAL IS THE ONLY CREATURE THAT HAS EVER KILLED OFF ENTIRE SPECIES OF OTHER ANIMALS." The sign is not mounted on one of the animal cages but below a mirror. . .since keeping humans in zoos is frowned upon.

You can live longer if you quit doing the things that make you want to.

Cooperation is doing with a smile what you planned to do anyway.

Tact is the ability to give someone a shot in the arm without him feeling the needle.

Don't ever be right at the wrong time.

Most of the time it's wrong to do "what we have a right to do."

Trust everybody, but cut the cards.

Hate and envy are weapons that man uses to cover up his own shortcomings.

If at first you succeed you probably haven't accomplished much.

The hardest fall a man can take is falling over his own bluff.

When you are old enough to care what people say about you, nobody says anything.

Little minds are hurt by little things.

To get along, sometimes you have to go along.

Too many people insult friends and flatter strangers.

Diplomacy is the art of saying "nice doggie" while you look for a big rock.

It may be "human to err," said Rover, "but a human don't have his nose rubbed in it and put outside."

Any time you think you have influence, just try ordering somebody else's dog around.

A school bus driver has all his troubles behind him.

God makes the world all over again when my grandson places his security blanket over me when I'm dozing on the couch.

Heaven will not be heaven if you do not meet your family there.

This would be a sad world without children and an inhuman world without the aged.

Grandparents are so simple that even a child can operate them.

Too many parents tie up their dog and let their children run loose.

Children often hold a marriage together. They keep their parents so busy they don't have time to quarrel.

The best pitch a little-leaguer has is one that reaches the plate.

A child is much more affectionate when he is eating chocolate candy and you have on your Sunday best.

To get maximum attention, it's hard to beat a great big boo-boo.

Smile! It's easy to be happy. Think, too! It's easy to be a smiling moron.

You have to test the odds. A man can't steal second with his foot on first.

America is a country of trust. On the installment plan you can buy what you can't afford, and on the stock market you can sell what you don't own.

Getting a bargain is the best way to give your garage mechanic plenty of business.

Car sickness is that feeling you get when the monthly payment is due.

Another sign of American progress is small cars and big lawn mowers.

Parking space is something that disappears while you make a U-turn.

A spare tire is the one that you carefully check after you've had a flat.

Luxuries are like a child's toys. They're more fun if there aren't too many of them.

Only in America does a man read a 200-page book to learn how to run around the block.

The rainy days for which a person saves usually come up during vacation.

A refrigerator is where you keep left-overs until they're old enough to throw out.

If you want to get real busy, start picking up the beans you've spilled.

You give things to people because you want them to like you.

The best way to live happily ever after is not to be after too much.

Save for all the rainy days you want, but enjoy today's sunshine, too.

Prosperity is buying things we don't want with money we don't have to impress people we don't like.

The most beautiful things in the world are the most useless. Peacocks and azaleas, for example.

As with business, the same with fish. The big ones eat up the little ones.

When a man sits down to wait for his ship to come in, it usually turns out to be a receiving ship.

A bill collector is a man who doesn't believe in putting off until tomorrow what can be dunned today.

Even a live wire has to have good connections.

The water in the well can not be purified by painting the pump.

Don't throw away your old pot until you're sure your new one will hold water.

When misfortune comes, you will find out which one of your friends was waiting with a paddle to catch you bent over.

The best safety device in a car is a rear view mirror. . .with a police car in it.

Once in every man's youth, there comes a time when he must learn that the world wasn't created just for his benefit.

Before you call yourself a peace-loving man, tell us how you act when the umpire calls a close one on the home team.

A man doesn't cut his wisdom teeth until he bites off more than he can chew.

Eat your bread and you will be fed. Share your bread and you will taste the flavor.

Chop your own wood. It will warm you twice.

All arrows of truth should be dipped in a little honey.

If you love your kids, belt them. . .in the car seat.

The six year old says that a kumquat is what you do when you call you Quat.

The unresolvable contradiction in the male nature is that no father wants his daughter to do what he wanted to do to somebody else's daughter.

There are no seven wonders of the world to children. In their eyes there are seven million.

No matter how much cats fight, there's always plenty of kittens.

When you borrow money from a friend, think which of the two you need the most.

America is the only country in the world where a person can have a $70,000 mortgage and still be called a home owner.

It's nice to walk to town. . .that is, if you own a car.

Ain't nothing more satisfying than parking on what's left of the other feller's dime.

Buying on time used to mean getting to the store before it closed.

Wealth is something that you cannot enjoy unless you have known poverty.

Many men who refuse to believe in Santa Claus are convinced they can beat the horses.

If you lend a friend $5 and you never see him again, it's worth it.

Watch those used cars. They're not what they are jacked up to be.

A money-grabber is anyone who can grab more money than you can grab.

Money is an instrument that can buy you everything but happiness and pay your fare to any place but heaven.

Money may not be everything, but you will have to admit that it's way ahead of what's second.

A conservative is someone who thinks nothing should be done for the first time.

It would seem that nowadays a congressman's term lasts until he is caught.

The scientists who got the lead out of our gas should start to work on Congress.

With love or politics, indifference is fatal.

There are two kinds of voters. Those who support your candidate and a lot of ignorant, prejudiced fools.

Politicians are like polkas. They all sound alike but have different names.

Doctors, as with lawyers; the less we have to do with them, the better.

Preachers, as with doctors; it's safer to get a second opinion.

More hearts hurt in secret from unkindness from those who should be comforters than from anything an enemy says.

Just because a man is not your enemy doesn't make him your friend.

Do your work and let your enemy alone; someone will come along some day and do him in for you.

A friend is someone who has the same enemies that you do.

One reason that we love our enemies is that they don't borrow anything.

When the other person acts that way, he's ugly. When you do, it's nerves.

Nobody ever forgets where he buried the hatchet.

You don't know what's good until you have tasted the bad.

The average man has five senses: touch, taste, sight, smell, and hearing. The successful man has two more: horse and common.

A bachelor is a man who missed the opportuntiy to make some woman miserable.

There are a few places where a harmless lie is a great deal better than a harmful truth.

Happiness is that period between too little and too much.

The best things in life are not things.

Isn't it strange how small annoyances divide people, and that major tragedies draw them together.

If there is so much hate in this world, how do you account for the population explosion?

Happiness is fine, but it takes grief to make a man.

An average man is one who thinks he isn't.

A good sport is anyone who will always let you have your own way.

Luck is always against the man who depends on it.

There is no disguise that can hide love where it exists, nor is there a way to fake it where it does not exist.

Whiskey is about the only enemy man has succeeded in really loving.

Alcohol is a liquid good for preserving almost everything except secrets.

Self-discipline is easy when there are no whiskey or women around.

The devil can quote scripture to suit his own purpose.

Good losers are usually just good actors.

Without some variety, no pleasure will last.

Some folks never get interested in anything until it's none of their business.

You never will meet a man so ignorant that you can't learn something from him.

Every time you graduate from the school of experience, someone thinks up a new course.

There is no medicine like hope; no incentive so great, and no tonic so powerful as the expectation of something tomorrow.

Nothing is as good as it seems beforehand.

A dab of horse sense is better than all the good luck charms put together.

A word of encouragement during a failure is worth more than a dictionary of praise after a success.

You shouldn't pray for rain, then complain about the mud.

What you don't know may not hurt you, but it can make you act mighty stupid.

Never send someone to clean out the attic who likes to read.

Some folks don't like the fan dancer. . .others don't like the fan.

A raving beauty is one who comes in second in a beauty contest.

There is no such thing as a little garlic.

The best birth control device is called "garlic."

Folks who like sausage and whiskey should never watch either being made.

An old-fashioned girl is now an endangered species.

A man's best fortune is his wife. . .or his worst.

How come girls' best friends are diamonds while man's best friend is an old dog? What's equal about that?

A man shouldn't run after a trolley or a woman; there will be another one along presently.

Whenever a girl meets a man who would make a good husband, he usually is.

You don't have to be a cook to know when the food is bad.

For every woman who makes a fool out of a man, there is another woman who makes a man out of a fool.

Some women dress as if they had no faith in a man's imagination.

Up until 20, a girl needs good parents. From 20 to 40, it's good looks. From 40 to 60 it's good humor. And from 60 up, good stocks and bonds.

Home is where some men go to raise hell because something went wrong at the office.

The difference between a happy marriage and an unhappy one is leaving about three or four things a day unsaid.

A man supporting two wives is not necessarily a bigamist. His son may be married.

In revenge, as in love, a woman is always more barbarous than man.

Wives never forget that they have forgiven.

The best labor-saving device for a woman is a devoted husband.

Nothing pleases a wife more than for her husband to ask for something he threw out the month before.

Housework is what a woman does that's never noticed unless she doesn't do it.

If you forgive a man, don't heat it up for breakfast.

Some women judge their husbands by the worst thing they hear about other men.

It's always the woman who had her hair done that day who has a question at the PTA meeting.

Brains are what you look for in a girl after you've looked at everything else.

The mechanical lie detector will never be as successful as the one made from Adam's rib.

How many times do you think these words are heard about 3:00 in the afternoon across the nation: "Good grief, are you home already?"

"I'm glad you brought that up" is as good an answer as you will get.

Whoever named it "necking" was a poor judge of anatomy.

Love is the delusion that one girl differs from another.

Laughter is a wordless kind of speech by which we express feelings we couldn't put in a thousand words.

If you want the winter to pass quickly, give your note to come due in the spring.

A well-informed man is one with opinions. . .just like your own.

There are many people who think Sunday is a sponge that wipes out all the sins of the week.

Where you go hereafter depends largely on what you go after here.

Most choirs in church would be very silent if no one sang there except the ones who sing best.

If you let the cat out of the bag, don't try to cram it back in. It only makes matters worse.

If "it goes without saying," why does everybody say it?

No matter what happens, there is always somebody who knew it would.

People who do the most for our community are the ones who demand the least.

We love folks here in the mountains, not for what they do or what they have, but simply because they are.

We wish that there were something left these days that could honestly be called "unmentionable."

My wife Geri has never told me the difference between "I told you so" and "I'm not going to say 'I told you so.' "

A banker is one of the few businessmen who don't profit from the needy. He won't lend money to anyone who needs it.

A cocktail party is a place where they spear olives and stab friends.

Never before have homes been so comfortable and families so seldom in them.

Everyone says forgiveness is a good idea. . .until they have someone to forgive.

There is no bond between men like the bond forged between two women who have shared a good cry.

Do not prepare the path for the youth; prepare the youth for the path.

Most of the people favoring birth control have already been born.

I know you believe you understand what you think I said, but I'm not sure you realize that what you heard is not what I meant.

A good spot remover is one which will remove the spot left by another spot remover.

For a better vacation, take half the clothes you figured on and twice the money.

It is as wrong to trust everybody as it is to trust nobody.

Life begins at forty, but so do arthritis, lumbago and the habit of telling things to the same person four times.

A doctor's office is where people go to get a flu shot — and get the flu.